Block, Delete, Move On

www.penguin.co.uk

it's not you, it's them

LalalaLetMeExplain

BANTAM PRESS

TRANSWORLD PUBLISHERS

Penguin Random House, One Embassy Gardens, 8 Viaduct Gardens, London SW11 7BW
www.penguin.co.uk

Transworld is part of the Penguin Random House group of companies
whose addresses can be found at global.penguinrandomhouse.com

First published in Great Britain in 2022 by Bantam Press
an imprint of Transworld Publishers

A CIP catalogue record for this book
is available from the British Library.

ISBN 9781787635234

Typeset in 10.6/14.3 pt Garamond MT
Design by Couper Street Type Co.
Printed and bound in China by C&C Offset Printing Co., Ltd.

The authorized representative in the EEA is Penguin Random House Ireland,
Morrison Chambers, 32 Nassau Street, Dublin D02 YH68.

Penguin Random House is committed to a sustainable
future for our business, our readers and our planet. This book
is made from Forest Stewardship Council® certified paper.

www.greenpenguin.co.uk

For my darling son: everything I do, I do it for you.

For my mum: I hope this makes you proud.
I could not have done it without you.

'And I can't trust this world to teach their sons how to treat my daughter, so I will raise her to be a sword, a spear, a shield.'

— Elizabeth Acevedo (@acevedowrites)

Contents

Preface

Have you ever seen the meme that says 'Raise your hand if you've been personally victimized by your own taste in men' and raised your hand? Then this book is for you. This is not a dating book that promises to find you a person to love; instead, it will help you spot the troublesome ones before it's too late. I'm giving you all the information I wish I'd had long before I started dating men. I come at this from both a professional and a personal perspective – I have accidentally become attached to, or gone on disastrous dates with, far too many crap men. And I am not alone. I started putting my dating and relationship advice out on Instagram anonymously in 2017 and, through word of mouth alone, my page grew exponentially. So many people who date cis men (men whose gender identity matches the one assigned at birth) could relate to my diabolical experiences with these time-wasting wallies.

I recently saw this statistic from the Derm Review: one in five men only wash their balls twice a week or less. This really doesn't surprise me. It's just another piece of information that contributes to the wealth of evidence showing us that having no option but to date men because of your sexuality is a curse. And to be quite honest, smelly willies are the least of our problems.

Have you tried to date men in the last five years, since the rise of the apps? If so, I think you will know exactly what I am talking about, and if not, then you've been extremely lucky.

I am not a man-hater by any stretch of the imagination – quite the opposite – but the fact is that dating is a mission. It can be hard work for everyone, but dating men in particular is a knobstacle course that requires up-to-date knowledge and intense training if you are to complete it safely.

I have made so many dating-related mistakes, like the time I sent a three-minute-long voice note and through floods of drunken tears explained to a guy I really liked that I had Daddy issues. Or the time when I went on a first – and last – date with someone who assaulted an elderly man in the street. Or the time when I unknowingly dated someone else's boyfriend for six months . . . I could write another twenty paragraphs on this, but you get the picture. I didn't know how to spot red flags, I didn't know how to filter out the bad guys, I didn't know how to conduct myself in a way that wasn't completely led by my heart and my desperate need to be loved.

I kept repeating a pattern: I'd meet a man who seemed really keen and intense to start with and we would fall into regularly seeing each other for months on end, at which point I would catch feelings and assume he was equally into me because of how often he came over. I'd spend our whole situationship asking him to make more effort, placing meaning on the times he fell asleep holding me and feeling frustrated that he could only fit me in during booty-call hours, not realizing that, in his mind, I was allocated only hook-up status. I would give him full relationship benefits and treat him like I would a partner, because I felt that it would show him how great it was to have me around and that eventually he would declare that he loved me. And sometimes they did. But I failed to recognize that these declarations of love didn't match their actions, and I always ended up hurt. It became a lifestyle, transforming myself into everything I thought I needed to be to make a man want me: a sexual freak (with no orgasms in return), a place for them to receive emotional solace after a hard day of selling weed, a taxi service after their nights out with mates that I was never invited to. It never occurred to me that I was making it easy for them to have their cake and eat it. I always dated with my heart rather than my head – in fact, I intentionally left my brain at the door and purposely put my body forward because I believed that it was the most valuable thing I had to offer.

My best friend was having issues with men too, but different ones. She was finding it easy to meet men who fell in love with her, but she was only dating men who needed fixing. Three months into their whirlwind love affair, she would be dealing with them having dramatic breakdowns, or moving in with her because they had found themselves homeless, or suddenly realizing that they had deep-rooted Mummy issues. And things weren't much better for my married friends: one was fleeing domestic violence while another three were holding down households and children while their husbands sank into mid-life crises, including cocaine and alcohol addiction.

In November 2016 I ended a relationship with the fuckboy who broke the camel's back. He was a narcissistic wasteman who managed to convince me that he was soon to be a millionaire, but, in the meantime, I had to top up his Oyster card if I wanted to see him. He was the latest failed romance in a string that had lasted since I started online dating in 2013. Before that, I had been in two back-to-back long-term relationships, the most recent being with the father of my son. We got together in 2006, our son was born in 2011 and I was a single parent from the day he was born. I didn't start dating again until my son was about eighteen months old. It was then that I discovered that things had drastically changed since the last time I was single. And I mean *drastically*. Men had changed. I had found it very easy to meet men who wanted relationships prior to the dawn of Tinder and Plenty of Fish, but since the birth of the apps, and with my new single-mum status, it felt like every man wanted one thing – to take me for an absolute mug.

After things ended with the fuckboy that broke the camel's back, I decided that I needed to work on myself. I got really into the Law of Attraction and learned more about my own spirituality, and it helped me to better understand myself and the ways I was behaving in relationships. I had all these epiphanies – it became clear to me why I was compromising myself in order to gain male validation. I had studied attachment theory for years, but it hadn't occurred to me to apply the principles to my own love life. I began to understand why my insecure attachment style was leading me to anxiously attach myself to these men. I began to see that I was waving some red flags myself and that I had been manipulative and controlling in a previous relationship. I had to force myself to sit with the discomfort of that knowledge and to figure out how to change it. I realized where I was going wrong.

But it was more than that. I'd studied feminism, misogyny and toxic masculinity in my social work degree, but my natural inclination to blame myself and internalize every rejection or any ill treatment I received made me fail to make the connection with what was happening to me. Looking at my friends who dated men, I realized that we were all facing a variety of problems that my male friends who dated women were rarely experiencing: like having scary first-date experiences, being used and ghosted after sex, being strung along in no-labels situations or becoming their unpaid carer/mother. I began to see that many of the problems I was experiencing were caused by virtue of my gender.

I realized that there is a definite problem with men and the way they treat women.

As individuals, there are some great men, but as a group there are some issues that need ironing out. I now understand that, until that happens, those of us who date them need to be fully equipped to deal with their audacity.

I should have noticed all this because I was working as a children and families social worker, with a first-class honours degree in the subject, and before that, I'd been a sexual health and relationships educator for the NHS, teaching in schools and youth settings. I was a qualified social work practice teacher too. I spent my near-twenty-year career supporting women to identify and leave abusive relationships, educating people about building healthier connections, supporting people trying to break toxic cycles and protecting families from harm. Yet I was going home and begging men who were treating me with ambivalence to love me better. I had always been able to give the best advice to others, but I struggled to apply it to my own love life.

For the first time ever, I decided that I needed to stop believing that a relationship was my biggest goal. I needed a clean break to unfuck myself. I reflected on everything I had learned about men and myself during the four years I had been online dating and it all started making sense to me. I invested all of the energy and attention I'd wasted on men into myself. I started loving myself and my own company. I stopped needing male attention and validation. I looked back over all the encounters I'd had online, and the patterns and the red flags became glaringly obvious. Once I had figured it out, I wanted to shout from the rooftops. I wanted all women to know that they had the power to really enjoy being single and to show them how to spot these red flags a mile off and be confident enough to block anyone exhibiting the tell-tale signs. That is what motivated me to start my Instagram page and blog, and it felt empowering to be connected to so many more women and people who date men who were also dealing with this shit. It became clear to me that we all need a bit of guidance as to how to tackle the current state of modern dating.

I am finally in a place of being completely content with being single, and I want this book to help others get there too. However, it feels important to state that this book was written during England's lockdown due to COVID-19, and for the first time in a long time I found myself wanting a man. It was a particularly difficult time for single people (and people stuck in horrible relationships) because it suddenly felt like perhaps we had missed the boat. The loneliness that so many of us had felt on Saturday nights when all of our friends were out with their partners became a daily reality. It made a lot of people realize that they *did* want a relationship and then it made them feel completely panicked about how that would ever be possible again, given that we were living through what felt like an apocalypse. Although we are moving out of that situation now (I hope), it still had a significant impact on dating in terms of that sense of lost time, so I hope that this book can take some of that panic away.

A caveat before we start. For the purposes of this book, when I refer to women, trans women are included in this. Trans women are women. However, when I refer to men in this book, I solely mean cisgender men. Trans men are men but, bar a few exceptions, most trans men aren't misogynists. They were socialized as girls/women and gained their perspective of life from the other side. I spoke to several trans men to establish whether this would feel exclusionary, and they all stated that they were happy not to be included in discussions about the toxic element of masculinity, because they tend not to perpetuate it. Misogyny has a huge impact on queer relationships too, particularly in the form of homophobia, and in creating pressure to conform to heterosexual ideals of gender roles within the relationship. Domestic violence is also commonplace in same-sex or non-gender-conforming couples. Dating and relationships can be hard for everyone – heterosexual men included. But my reason for focusing specifically on the experiences of heterosexual women who date cisgender men is because that is what I know. I would rather LGBTQI+ experiences were represented by LGBTQI+ writers. I don't think it's my place to speak about issues on behalf of LGBTQI+ people, so I would rather pass the mic to people like Lindsay King-Miller (author of *Ask a Queer Chick: A Guide to Sex, Love and Life for Girls Who Dig Girls*), Jo Langford (author of *The Pride Guide*) and Jamie Windust (author of *In Their Shoes*). While some parts of this book are quite gender-specific, it is my hope that many parts are relevant to everyone, no matter how you identify and no matter who you date. However, the chapters about sex (Chapters 7 and 8) do use specific biological language around penises and vaginas. This may feel triggering to people who are not cisgender. I chose to use this type of language because the orgasm gap is very specific to cis-het women who sleep with cis-het men. However, I invite anyone to apply my advice to their own situation if it feels relevant, regardless of the gendered language used in the book. I don't want my focus on heterosexual women's issues in dating and relationships to be taken as a dismissal of all the shitty things that other people experience.

This book is for anyone who has felt lost, confused, exhausted, drained or deflated by dating. It is for anyone who has laid in bed at night wondering whether they should text someone who has been treating them like shit. It is for anyone who has wondered if there is something wrong with them because a fuckperson can't see their value, for anyone who jumps on the apps with hope every six months and then deletes them a week later because they are exhausting.

You are not alone.

This is the anti-fuckperson guidebook, born out of my terrible dating experiences, my professional knowledge and what I have learned from all of the wonderful people who have shared stories with me on my Instagram over the years. I want you to know that if you're going through some stuff – if you've been hurt, humiliated, coerced in bed, ghosted, lied to, abused – whatever it is that you've been through in the dating Wild West, you need to know there are thousands who have been through the same and survived it. In my Instagram community, you have a literal army behind you. I guarantee you that if I posted your story, you would have tens of thousands of people sending you support and feeling genuine love for you. You would have thousands of people wanting to tell you that they have been through the same, and that things will get better and that we are all behind you. Painful times can feel really lonely: I want this book to remind you that you are not alone. We're all in this together, and we've got you. I want this book to make you feel that singleness is fantastic and that there is no need to chase love, but I am also assuming that you are reading a dating book because you want a partner at some point. So, while being contentedly single is the main goal here, there is no shame in knowing that you want a companion and in using this book to date in a healthier way with a well-honed red-flag radar. This is your fuckboy filter.

Chapter 1:

Not all men, but way too many

I matched a guy on Hinge, he's great on paper and we seem to get on well. However, when we followed each other on social media I discovered that he is following a lot of Alpha Male dating advice pages. He has also reshared some really worrying posts, including one with a guy advising men to give women the silent treatment if they withhold sex, and a meme about choking women if they nag too much. He seems like such a sweet guy, but his social media is 90% misogynistic memes and posts. Is this always a red flag?

love men. Lovely, kind, funny, brilliant, decent blokes. I adore them. There are millions of good ones: if there weren't, I would have just called my Instagram (IG) page 'Giveupandwank' and focused it all on dating yourself. But there are far too many bad ones. There are bad women too: evil, manipulative, controlling women – millions of them. The difference is that men don't need to alter their daily lives to protect themselves from those women. Women have to take precautions because of men. Every day. Everywhere in the world. Of course, not all men are dangerous, but everyone who presents as a woman has to fear men; every single woman in the world has to be cautious. We have to cover our drinks in bars, send our locations to friends when we go on dates, take cabs instead of public transport after midnight, carry our keys between our fingers when we go for walks alone, all because of 'not all men'. It's far too many men. Even the men who say 'Not all men' at every opportunity warn their own daughters and wives to be wary of other men.

> There is not a man alive who doesn't know that it is unsafe for women to do certain things because of men.

They might argue that it's not always safe for boys and men either, and they would be right. But it's not women who are posing that risk; boys and men also need to be worried about men. (This is exactly why men need to get on board as allies; it benefits men to end male violence and toxic masculinity as much as it benefits women.) Men who date men also need to be careful; men can be scary when dating other men too. There is little evidence to suggest that anyone who dates women needs to be wary of physical or sexual violence on a first date (however, it can happen). Queer women should also be warned that sometimes creepy men pose as women on dating apps, so caution is always advised.

But even though I love men, they have also been the bane of my life. I spent many years occupying this world as a cisgender heterosexual woman without really considering what that meant, or how it impacted on how I was viewed and treated and on what I thought my role should be and how I was expected to behave. I never really thought about it. I never gave my experiences context. The thousands of times, since childhood, that I was shouted at by men in the street letting me know they wanted to 'suck my tits'. The countless times I was flashed or wanked at in the street or on public transport, which also started when I was a child. The many times I had my bum groped by passing men in raves, or a man pressed too close to me on the Tube. The times boys at school grabbed my breasts and laughed about it. The times men on dating apps initiated conversation with vulgar demands on my body. The times when I put up with things that hurt in bed because I wanted to be wanted. The countless times I have put myself through pain from waxing, or walking in heels that cut, because I thought I needed to look a certain way to be attractive to men. The times when I have felt intimidated or scared with someone who should have made me feel safe.

I blamed myself for those times. I just kind of accepted that I was a bit unlucky, that maybe I had something about me that made men think they could do or say incredibly fucked-up things to me.

That maybe I was putting out an energy that was provoking men to sexually objectify me.

I looked for reasons within myself to explain why I was attracting shitty behaviour, but internalizing it made me think less of myself, which then led me to tolerate more from men because I didn't believe that I deserved better. I also minimized bad behaviour; I knew that some things, like being groped at school, were happening to lots of girls, so, instead of being horrified by a boy lifting up my skirt to touch my knickers, I just thought it was normal, and you couldn't say anything because it was only a joke.

I made absolutely no link to misogyny. Because of the various tropes that were around when we were growing up, I was led to believe that boys are mean to you if they like you, while the boys were being told that girls play hard to get so they should pursue us even if we tell them we're not interested. We're told that girls mature faster than boys, which inevitably removes accountability and agency from boys and places it all on girls.

These experiences with men also made me really dislike other women because I saw them as competition. I was a 'pick me' girl: a woman who holds internalized misogyny. She centres herself in the male gaze and makes sexist statements as a way of proving that she is better than other girls, thereby encouraging men to pick her. 'Pick me' women conform to patriarchal ideals of womanhood despite that not being true to who they really are. They see other women as opponents so view them with mistrust. As a result of their low self-esteem, they try to assert superiority over other women by conforming to rigid gender norms that appeal to misogynistic men, like the trope of the silent, subservient wife. She is not a woman who takes a submissive role because she really loves it while also having respect for the choices other women make; she is a woman who compromises her own needs in order to appeal to men and throws other women under the bus in pursuit of them. Just look in the comments section under a sexy Instagram picture of any female celebrity who has been cheated on and you will find 'pick me's in there, making critical judgements: 'I'm not being funny, but maybe he cheated because she's always going out and posting sexy pictures!'

I used to engage in this behaviour because I wanted to be wanted by men. Their approval was very important to me. Now I am proud to be like other women because I know that we're all in this together.

Millions of women across the world will tell you that the first time they remember being subject to the male gaze and feeling sexually objectified was when they were a child. I vividly recall a time when my mum, then aged forty-two, was telling a friend that she had noticed that when we walked down the street together she no longer faced stares and catcalls from men because their attention had been turned to me. I was twelve. I remember being fifteen and not being able to walk down the street without being chatted up by men in cars. They would pull up alongside me as I walked, like kerb crawlers.

Of course, not every girl has those experiences growing up, but most women will have a similar story to tell about vile male behaviour at some point in their lives. We are all raised with the same cultural narratives – that when men do bad things to women, it is because the women brought it on themselves. That we need men to protect us, even though the only thing we need protecting from is men themselves. That we have to look and behave a certain way to be deemed attractive to men and that, if we're not, then we will probably fail at life because we won't be picked for marriage and babies and we will have no one to protect us. I've gone through life being told that if I want to find a husband, I should downplay my intelligence; that I should swear less; that I might intimidate men if I'm too successful so I shouldn't aspire to be. I've been told that I should emphasize the fact that I can cook and that I go to the gym but downplay the number of men I've slept with. We're all told this. But while we're being told all this, we're also experiencing something different. As I mentioned above, from a tragically young age most girls will begin getting attention from men – catcalls, wolf whistles, sleazy remarks and gropes from boys in school. Stuff that doesn't feel right, but we don't realize we're allowed to call it out because we see it everywhere and it's 'just banter' and it's what happens to girls. We begin to feel validated by it. And then, as we grow, it continues. Images of women in magazines and videos are generally ultra-sexualized and porn culture is everywhere: we learn that to fully attract men's attention we have to be sexy. Men tell us how desirable we are to get us into bed and then they judge and devalue us for using the thing that they taught us was most valuable.

The Madonna/whore complex is a sad reality for some.

> Many men can't see women as whole humans who can coexist as a healthy partner and potential mother who also loves sex; it's one or the other for them.

They desire the 'whore' but don't respect her because they can't control her and because she is 'tainted' by other men, while they can respect the virgin because they consider her 'pure'.

The bar is set so high for women. We are taught that we have to match up to all of these ideals to be deemed attractive by men who have managed to be so consistently crap over the years that the dating and relationships bar for them is on the floor. How many times have we praised men for not trying it on with us on a first date? As though they are such restrained gentlemen for not groping us. Or rung our girlfriends to tell them we're going to marry him because he focused on our pleasure and made sure we came before he did. *That's what men are supposed to do.* When people find out that I am a single mother, one of the first things they ask is whether the dad is involved, and when I say that he is people nearly always remark that it's so good that he's around. Nobody has ever praised me for sticking around to raise my son, there are no special accolades for doing what is expected of you as a mother, yet people want to hand out trophies because a man takes his kids to McDonald's every other Sunday? Get the fuck out of here. Even when we raise our children together, fathers will be applauded for 'babysitting' their own kids or 'helping out' around the home. Expectations of them are so basic, even when it comes to clothes and presentation. We wear uncomfortable shoes or clothes or restrictive underwear or have extreme beauty treatments, all for men who roll up in comfortable jumpers and battered-looking trainers. It's all so imbalanced.

In her compelling and comprehensive book *Everyday Sexism*, Laura Bates explains how the insidious messaging about women and girls that is fed to us by the media and seeps into social attitudes has a huge impact on us. She highlights things like the ITV morning show *Daybreak* holding a debate in 2013 asking whether women who get drunk and flirt are to blame if they are attacked. Or the Channel 5 TV show *The Wright Stuff* holding an opinions segment on whether men pinching women's bottoms in nightclubs is 'just a bit of fun'. This was in response to a campaign group that was trying to persuade nightclubs to commit to expelling men who groped women. A female celebrity panellist exclaimed that groping in nightclubs is 'harmless' and then blamed it on the fact that women wear very little in clubs these days. Nobody can ever be to blame for sexual assault apart from the person doing the assaulting – yet our mainstream media are pushing narratives that suggest otherwise.

I had my first epiphany when I started studying social work and I began to understand that this was a systemic problem. I was witnessing first hand the huge volume of women and children who had been through the same things as me, and far worse. I saw women of all ages, classes and ethnicities being treated in all sorts of harmful ways by men – and the way that those intersections impacted women's experiences differently. At the same time, I was learning about feminism and reading books by women like bell hooks, the notable Black feminist writer, and author and journalist Naomi Wolf, and it all began to make more sense. It really sank in that sexism and oppression were societal problems and that I was a victim of the way society was set up. I started to understand that the issue was the patriarchy, not me. That it was a systemic problem, not a personal one, and one that harms everyone – including men – to varying degrees by virtue of their class, ethnicity or background. 'The patriarchy was designed to uphold men first and white women second,' says Kelechi Okafor, actor, director and businesswoman. 'Black women have historically been left out of the narrative – for example, look at romance films: the Black chick is always side-lined as the best friend rather than

I started to understand that the issue was the *patriarchy* NOT ME the love interest. Black women are seen as strong and self-sufficient, so not deserving of love or protection.' This is misogynoir – a term coined by Moya Bailey to describe the anti-Black sexism Black women face. We see this across other cultures too – think about how Asian women are perceived as submissive and are overly sexualized, or how Muslim women can sometimes be controlled by some of the more misogynistic aspects of their culture 'while also experiencing a very specific type of Islamophobia and control from white women who want to fight against burqas or hijabs, under the guise of feminism', says Munira, from @muslimsexeducation on Instagram. Class is a huge factor too: think about how the victims of grooming gangs in Rochdale – mainly working-class white girls – were failed by everyone who was supposed to protect them because they weren't deemed worthy. Assumptions were made about how working-class girls behaved and the sense was that they created their own vulnerabilities. All women are at risk of male violence by virtue of their gender, but ethnicity, class, sexuality and disability increase vulnerability and reduce access to protection.

Rape, sexual assault and violence against women and girls (VAWG) is a certified and recognized problem in every country in the world and most have specific VAWG policies to address the issue. The World Health Organization (WHO) has recognized it as a significant public health concern.[1] The statistics and evidence show that women are at risk of physical and sexual violence and domestic homicide because of men and that it's an issue underpinned by misogyny, the patriarchy, male privilege, toxic masculinity, gender roles and a male sense of entitlement and ownership over women and our bodies. From the United Nations to the WHO to the UK government, everyone uses the abbreviation VAWG,

---

1   Topping, Alexandra. 'Four-fifths of young women in the UK have been sexually harassed, survey finds'. The *Guardian*, 10 March 2021 (amended 24 March 2021). https://www.theguardian.com/world/2021/mar/10/almost-all-young-women-in-the-uk-have-been-sexually-harassed-survey-finds 2021).

but this removes agency from the men who are perpetuating this violence in the first place, so the term should be *Male* violence against women and girls: MVAWG.

> So, when 'Gary' jumps into conversations about rape or domestic violence to defend men's honour by letting us know that not *every single* man in the world is a danger to women, he just sounds like a dickhead.

We all know that it's not *all* men, but it is enough that governments need whole strategies and task forces to address it. It's enough that 71 per cent of women have experienced sexual harassment (the remaining 29 per cent possibly don't realize that catcalling is harassment; I don't think there is a woman alive who hasn't had comments from strangers).[2] It's enough men that two women a week are murdered by their partner or ex-partner in England and Wales alone. It's enough men that one in three women will experience domestic abuse in her lifetime.[3] It's enough men that a woman is raped every six minutes. Ninety per cent of sexual assaults are committed by men who know the woman they are harming,[4] so it's enough men that we have to be careful of the men closest to us. It's too many men. Of course, men are also victims of domestic violence, but the disparity arises when it comes to sexual violence and murder. So when Gary says, 'What about men? This happens to us too,' the facts don't lie: we are simply not killing and raping men at epidemic levels.

Recently, I did some polls on my page, and nearly 10,000 women responded (2 per cent of respondents were men). Sixty-five per cent of

---

2   https://www.theguardian.com/world/2021/mar/10/almost-all-young-women-in-the-uk-have-been-sexually-harassed-survey-finds

3   'Devastatingly pervasive: 1 in 3 women globally experience violence'. WHO newsletter, 9 March 2021. https://www.who.int/news/item/09-03-2021-devastatingly-pervasive-1-in-3-women-globally-experience-violence

4   Bates, Laura. *Everyday Sexism* (London, 2014).

respondents said they had been sexually assaulted, yet 91 per cent said that they had been sexually groped in a public place, such as a bar or a festival. That's a 26 per cent disparity, meaning a quarter of the people who responded had normalized being groped to the point where they didn't even consider it to be sexual assault. Seventy-nine per cent said that it was common in secondary school for boys to sexually touch girls (including pulling bra straps, slapping bottoms, and so on) and that everyone saw it as a joke, or something that just happens to girls.

In *Misjustice: How British Law is Failing Women*, QC Helena Kennedy explains:

> *The law mirrors society with all its imperfections and it therefore reflects the subordination and lesser status of women, even today . . . The law is symbolic, playing an important role in the internalizing of ideas about what is right and natural. If the men of the law say scantily dressed women or ones who are drunk or ones who hook up with guys on Tinder have been authors of their own misfortune, they reinforce that view in the man on the street. The law constructs beliefs about the roles of men and women in the home and at work which feed back into generally held attitudes about women.*

You see it all over social media, in comments sections on posts about news stories featuring rape or sexual assault. There will be a worrying number of men chiming in to suggest that it's more likely that the woman is lying than it is that the man raped her, despite the fact that a man is 230 times more likely to be raped by another man than he is to be falsely accused of rape.[5] On a post about a footballer being charged with rape after a woman hooked up with him at 4 a.m. on a dating app, a woman commented, 'What did she think she was going to a footballer's house

---

5   Lee, Georgina. 'Men are more likely to be raped than be falsely accused of rape'. Channel 4 FactCheck, 12 October 2018. https://www.channel4.com/news/factcheck/factcheck-men-are-more-likely-to-be-raped-than-be-falsely-accused-of-rape

at 4 a.m. for? A sleepover? If you don't want to get raped, then don't put yourself in those situations' (perfect example of a 'pick me'). These people end up on juries, and that is partly why rape and sexual assault convictions are so low. Women and girls see this. We see how the law works. We see what people think of women who are harmed by men and so, from a very young age, we internalize it and normalize it. We don't seek protection and justice because we are very rarely afforded it, especially if you are not white.

When you realize that, as a heterosexual woman, you have no choice but to date people who might well be contributing to, upholding or directly causing all of this bullshit, it is a lightbulb moment. It was for me, anyway. I was fighting against the effects of misogyny and misogynoir at work on a daily basis. I was dealing with domestic violence, sexual abuse and exploitation day in, day out. But I was naively failing to attribute any of the stuff I was experiencing with the men I was dating to the wider context of sexism. Stuff like being pressured for nudes and being belittled or made fun of if you didn't want to send them. Or being seduced into bed with the promise of a long-term relationship, but that promise dissolving after sex.

> That feeling of knowing deep down that you don't want to do something but finding yourself worrying that perhaps you should because you don't want to hurt his feelings or let him down; you don't want to disappoint him, or make him angry.

So many of us have been in these kinds of scary situations with someone who we thought was safe. We don't want to be verbally or physically assaulted or have to flee from his flat. We worry that it's our fault because that's the narrative we're given: that we led him on, that we were a 'cock tease', and that we have to go through with it now because we've come this far.

The #MeToo movement created by Tarana Burke highlighted issues of power and exploitation and helped a lot of women to realize that they

IT'S A

CYCLE,

AND WE

PERPETUATE

IT WHEN

WE DATE

MEN WHO

UPHOLD

THIS SHIT.

were not alone. It empowered women and encouraged us to speak. The rise in women telling their stories since the #MeToo movement began has been phenomenal. It has inspired a new generation of feminists to start fighting, but it has also created a backlash from defensive men. There is an abundance of misogyny disguised as 'banter' all over social media. For every woman reading a #MeToo-inspired story that resonates with her and realizing that she was not at fault in her own experiences, there is another poisonous slut-shaming post online being read by a fourteen-year-old girl who has just been groped and who now thinks that she is to blame, or a boy who thinks it's 'jokes' to touch girls without consent. It's a cycle, and we perpetuate it when we date men who uphold this shit.

Let me make it very clear that in no way do I hold women responsible for men's behaviour. However, when we tolerate it, we allow it to fester and breed.

> Dating men who hold sexist beliefs is like someone from a marginalized group dating a fascist. It is dangerous and toxic.

We can see that clearly. Why is it so much harder to see that dating men who believe that they are superior to women, or who slut-shame women for doing things they praise men for, or who post rape jokes on social media, is just as ludicrous and unsafe? A lot of women will end up dating men who hold sexist attitudes (in differing degrees) and a lot of times we end up subconsciously conforming to those attitudes. We mould ourselves into being the woman he wants us to be rather than the woman we are.

But who we are, deep down in our core, is usually a pretty amazing woman, and to diminish that for the sake of some grotbag who believes that he is superior to you by virtue of his gender is an insult to your mother's vagina. She did not endure painful childbirth for you to dim your light for somebody's dickhead of a son. We have to challenge this at every turn.

*

Feminism began in order to fight for equality for women. However, feminism is not a worthy cause unless it is intersectional (a term coined by Kimberlé Williams Crenshaw) and includes anyone who identifies as a woman. A lot of people shy away from describing themselves as feminists, because it has become a dirty word. You will hear people saying that they believe in equality but they don't believe in feminism because it's a political movement that intends to make women superior to men, but they are wrong. Some women will avoid the term because it is off-putting to men, some of whom think that a feminist is a bra-burning man-hater. They are wrong too. You can be a feminist without subscribing to any particular brand or wave of feminism. You can enjoy rough sex and cater to your man and still be a feminist – so long as you are doing those things because you want to, not because you feel you have to. You can fight for equality without that meaning you have to live by set-in-stone principles of feminism. And you can definitely be a feminist and love men – part of being a feminist is wanting things to be better for them too.

> To me, feminism is simply the belief that women should be entitled to live as freely as men without our rights being restricted by laws, systems or indeed dangerous men.

Having said that, there is nothing wrong with not wanting to call yourself a feminist, as long as you aren't against the idea that women need a political movement that seeks to fight for equality. If you're on board with that, then you can call it whatever you want. Dating men who don't believe you should have equal rights across the board is wildly problematic. Yet the vast majority of us will have dated men who hold negative views about us without even considering the implications of this, and that needs to change. Unfortunately,

We can break the curse by refusing to accept less than what we deserve.

when a refusal to date men who secretly think that women are inferior becomes one of your non-negotiables, it becomes far harder to date. Asking men for their view on feminism within the first few messages on Tinder and the like works as a great filter.

Knowing all of this shouldn't terrify us – it gives us the power to understand that this is what we might face while dating. Heterosexuality can feel like a curse (though I'm not saying that being LGBTQI+ is any easier), but we can break the curse by refusing to accept less than what we deserve and by acknowledging that it's not us, it's misogyny. Making that link helps us to see not only that we deserve better but also that our actions aren't the cause of these problems. In terms of the fuckery that I have covered in this chapter – a depressing history of the failings of men and how that impacts on dating – it's definitely not us, it's them. Recognizing signs of misogyny and sexism is a big protective factor in avoiding controlling and abusive relationships. We must not underestimate the link between gender-based violence and abuse, so we must **block, delete and move on** at even the tiniest hint of it.

Chapter 2:

Spectacularly single buff ting

I'm 29 and perpetually single. I have been on the dating apps on and off for years, but I just cannot seem to meet a man who wants a relationship. I just don't know what I am doing wrong. Is it me? I'm desperate to find someone to settle down with, and it's making me miserable, especially because relatives keep asking why I'm still single. They are making me feel panicky about running out of time.

I hate being asked why I am single. I was born single, but if you could see the quality of men that we have to wade through on dating sites, then you might understand. Even the connotations around the word 'single' are annoying – it suggests that you are alone without a romantic partner – and terms like 'finding your other half' are even more annoying because you really can be whole and feel whole without one. We never ask attached people, 'Why are you in a relationship?' We just live under this weird assumption that, no matter what, being in a couple is preferable to not being in one.

We don't feel the need to ask couples to justify their status, so why do we ask singles?

It's a sensitive and potentially triggering question. Does anyone really need to explain that they are single because they're traumatized following an abusive relationship? Or that everyone they meet turns out to only be after sex? Or that they can't get past a second date without the other person disappearing? Or that they have issues that are messing with their ability to trust anyone? Sometimes these are the answers, and the fact that anyone thinks they have the right to demand these answers is, quite frankly, entitled and rude.

'So why are you single?' Sometimes the answer is simply because I adore my own company and I know my worth and I'm not willing to settle until I meet someone who I completely fit with, so I'm not going to compromise myself by forcing it with someone who only half fits. Sometimes the answer is because I don't feel that being single limits my life in any way, so I am not rushing to change that. It's okay to be single just because you're single, even if that goes on for ever. But it doesn't always feel like that, especially when all your friends are in relationships and you are the perpetually single one. Or when men on dating apps ask questions like 'What is a woman like you doing on an app like this?', as if to suggest that there must be something wrong with you for not having found love yet.

I remember when I first became interested in boys. I don't think I was actually particularly interested in *them*, I think I had just watched films like *Grease*, *Dirty Dancing*, *Heartbreak High* and *The Little Mermaid* so often that I assumed my next natural step in life was to be chosen by a boy so that we could get married and have babies (aged eleven). Little girls often aspire to be a wife; they dream about the day they are going to get married. How many boys do you know who grow up dreaming about their wedding day? It's no surprise, then, that when boys and older men started showing an interest in me, it felt like I was finally worthy. In secondary school, it really *meant* something to have a boyfriend or to receive a Valentine's card: your popularity rested on it. Being popular with boys meant you were popular with girls, so it was desirable to be in a couple at all times, even if being in a relationship literally just meant exchanging mix tapes, talking to each other on your house phone for hours and snogging with wildly over-enthusiastic tongues after school.

My desire to have a boyfriend in my late teens and early twenties was stronger than my desire to study, to focus on my goals or to carve out a decent career. In fact, my goals were all boy-related; none of them hinged on me doing anything with my own life apart from finding a man to share it with. I spent most of my spare time working on my looks in order to be as attractive to men as possible. Male attention made me feel good, and society told me that my value rested on whether I had been picked by one. It seemed obvious to me that I wasn't complete unless I had a boyfriend and so I wanted to have one at all times.

When I was a teenager in the nineties we didn't have the benefit of positive feminist social media accounts letting us know that it's okay to be single, we didn't have tweets spelling out the importance of self-love, we didn't have Google at our fingertips for advice. We just had popular culture letting us know that love, sex and marriage were the most important things in the entire world and that if we didn't have them, it was probably because we were too ugly or we were doing something wrong. *Sex and the City* had a huge impact on me. I loved it, and it glamorized being single (as long as you were relentlessly dating at all times). There is an episode in *SATC* where Charlotte says, 'Maybe our girlfriends are our soulmates and guys are just people to have fun with,' and that resonated with me. But, like me and my friends at the time, the women in *SATC* spent their entire friendship talking about the men they were having fun with. And often, that 'fun' didn't really feel like fun at all. It felt like constant stress. Stress about whether they liked us, stress about whether they would call us, stress about whether they were seeing other women, stress about ageing and gaining weight and the impact that might have on our ability to attract men.

> **Being single never felt fun and liberating, it felt like an affliction.**

Most of the girls I knew were on a permanent mission to find a man. If I went to a party or a bar and there were no eligible men, I would feel that it was a waste of time being there. For me, a night out when I was single was successful only if I got a phone number. I had no methods for being able to boost my own self-esteem. I was completely reliant on male attention for that, so being single always made me feel unworthy. I realize now that co-dependency was a factor here too, but I will cover that in more detail in Chapter 3.

For me, the pressure not to be single came from my own internalization of society's view that to be a great woman you had to be standing behind a great man (my past self makes me want to vomit), but for a lot of women this pressure comes from other sources too. One of the hardest things is loneliness. Loneliness is a feeling rather than an actual physical state. You can be with a group of friends and still feel lonely if you don't feel seen, heard or understood. Often, we feel at our loneliest when we are going through something we feel those around us don't understand; you can be in a room full of people and feel completely alone. Conversely, you can spend weekends entirely by yourself and not feel lonely at all. But when you're feeling crap about being single and you have it in your head that the only thing missing from your life is a partner, then it's very hard for that not to translate into feeling lonely on Saturday nights when all of your friends are out with their partners or when you're the only single one around the dinner table. Yet your friend sitting there with her husband could feel lonelier than anyone else – she could have suffered her third miscarriage and be feeling that nobody understands; she could feel distanced from her husband because she feels that he cares less about their loss than she does. You just don't know. The point is, the answer to loneliness is not a romantic relationship. In fact, you'd be better off getting a dog or a cat than a boyfriend in most cases. Talk about how lonely you feel with a counsellor or in an online group for loneliness or with friends. Talk it through. Your loneliness is far more likely to feel eased when you reach out for support than by desperately trying to date someone who can fill the void.

In most societies, it is taken as a given that a woman's role in life is to become a mother and a wife. Many girls are raised knowing that it would bring shame to their family if they choose another route. Women are often faced with constant questions from relatives about why they don't have a partner and with warnings to hurry up and find one before being 'left on the shelf' – a statement that really emphasizes how much power is given to men in the pursuit of relationships; we are simply objects sitting waiting to be picked, while our packaging declines in appeal the longer we are left in the shop window.

Grandmothers and aunties across the world have made their granddaughters feel like shit at family gatherings by questioning their single status and suggesting that they should change themselves in some way or another to be more attractive to potential husbands (advice can include dulling your achievements so as not to emasculate your partner; losing weight to make you appear more attractive;

you'd be better off getting a dog or a cat than a boyfriend in most cases becoming quieter and more docile so as not to be branded 'loud and annoying'). They very rarely say the same to their grandsons. No matter how much people tell you that being single is just as wonderful as being in a relationship, if you have been raised in a family whose ability to be proud of you rests on whether you get married and have babies, then it is not easy to feel that you can thrive proudly in your singleness. Pressure like this can make being single feel like an embarrassing reflection of everything you are lacking. Families with these expectations make being single feel like a failure. There are women with a Ph.D. who own their own property outright, but their family will still make them feel unsuccessful if they haven't managed to bag a man. It's a lot to contend with.

It's even harder if you are someone who knows that they want children, which is completely valid. Lots of women don't, and that is totally valid too.

> Motherhood does not define us as women, and if we don't ever have children, we are no less than women who do; we aren't less successful or less important, we haven't missed an essential part of life.

For every woman who feels pain at the thought of not being able to have a child, there is a woman who has had children with the wrong person who is deeply regretting it. We don't often hear from women whose truth is that they wish they hadn't had their children, because it's hard to say that out loud, but it is more common than we think. Womanhood is inherently linked with motherhood by society and so it often becomes our goal, simply because we feel that not producing offspring means that we have not completed life. Often, we choose to have children because we think we are supposed to, rather than because we absolutely love the idea of devoting our entire lives to raising another human. The latter really is the only reason that you should have children. You are no less of a woman and you have lived no less of a life if you choose not to have them or end up not having them. But for those of us who are certain that having children is important to us, the pressure of biology is, quite literally, a motherfucker.

It is very hard to relax into your singleness when it feels like you have a time limit before your opportunity to have children is taken away. This becomes particularly pressing when you reach your late thirties and you still haven't found anyone to start a family with. It can lead to us dating out of sheer desperation, then settling for whoever comes along. It can make us want to rush things with inappropriate men because we fear that they will be our last chance. This is also relevant to women who already have children but are keen to have more. It is such a nuanced discussion, and not one that can be tackled in a few paragraphs. I would recommend following the work of the wonderful Melanie Notkin, who is a leading voice for women who are childless not by choice. It is also worth looking into the options for having children alone. Some people know that they don't want children without a traditional family structure, but some know that they want children under any circumstances. If you have a good support network and a strong desire to go it alone, then you really don't need a man to help you raise your child. There are alternatives, like sperm donation, adoption, fostering, and so on, and it's important to look into your options. I know that the alternatives don't always take away the sense of loss and grief that is experienced by many women who feel that their dreams of pregnancy and/or a family will never be realized. It can be a huge thing that can feel much like a bereavement, and it is something that should not be underestimated when we sit here spouting about how we need to embrace being single.

But even with all of these very real pressures that can contribute to singledom feeling like a curse, embrace being single we must, because the only element that we have full control of is our mindset. It took me a long time to get into a headspace where I didn't feel that being single was a reflection of my unworthiness and where I wasn't constantly on the apps, looking for men to validate me. The change for me came after a rough break-up. Instead of reverting to my usual pattern of seeking attention to make me feel better, I forced myself to go completely man-free. I **blocked, deleted and moved on** from all the apps and people who I had been talking to, and put all of my focus into me.

> **There was something powerful about taking control.**

I was choosing to be single, and the longer it went on, the better being single felt. Going from feeling that being single is an affliction to embracing it as a positive choice is a journey that comes with regular wobbles, though. From my experience, I have identified four distinct phases of singleness.

Single and content

During this phase I am just not bothered about attracting a partner. I am busy, I spend time with my friends. I enjoy the opportunity to Netflix and chill on my own at weekends. I get a lot of work done. I sleep spread-eagled in my bed, content in the knowledge that I'm not currently being taken for a fool by some dusty grotbag. I feel satisfied knowing that a good partner will come if the universe decides to send one to me, but I am content because I know that I do not need a man to make my life any better than it already is. I feel like a **spectacular buff ting** and I bask in my fuckboy-free glow, safe in the knowledge that single is better than settling. I am open to talking to men, but I don't freak out about things not working out. I remember that the reason I'm not getting to a first date with anyone is because my filter is now fantastic, so I am spotting red flags early on. I am also not willing to waste my time on something that I know won't go anywhere so I'm not chatting mindlessly to people who don't stimulate me. I practise self-love and self-care and I feel satisfied with the relationship I have with myself.

Single and freaking out

This phase usually hits about a week before my period is due. I don't necessarily feel like I want or need a man, but I start wondering why none of them want or need me. A troll will say something in my comments, suggesting that I'm not capable of giving dating advice because I am single. Or they'll say, 'There are lots of good men, but they are all happily married to emotionally stable women, which is why you're still single,' and even though I know that this is the biggest load of nonsense (I know some incredibly emotionally unstable women in unhappy marriages), it still gets to me. Or a friend will announce an engagement or a relative a pregnancy and it sparks something off in me. It makes me worry that maybe being single is a bit shit. It makes me start wondering why it is that I can't seem to find anyone to text me back and whether there is actually something inherently wrong with me that is making men run away after approximately eight WhatsApp messages or place me in the sex-only zone before even meeting me. I start to feel ugly and old and I question everything about myself. I wonder whether it's my looks or my personality that I need to change in order to make someone want me. I see women who I have followed for a year on Insta on their third relationship in that short time, and I think, 'You've had three boyfriends in twelve months and I don't even have anybody to drunk text!' It makes me begin to question whether I need to lower my standards a bit. Or I'll see people who are still with their high-school sweethearts and I'll worry about why I didn't just make the sensible decision to have four babies with one boring man and be done with it. I hear friends say things like 'My mum has been single since my dad left in 1985' and I think, 'Fuck my life, maybe this is going to be me.' Thankfully, this phase is usually *very* brief.

Single and ready to mingle

After freaking out about the fact that I could remain single for the next forty years, I tell myself that this is ridiculous. I remind myself that while loving being single is great, it's also okay to know that you would like companionship and intimacy at some point in the future, so being open to it is a good thing. I remind myself that the Law of Attraction can only drop a man into my universe if I actually leave my house, or at least put some effort into trying to find someone. So, despite absolutely hating dating apps, I'll sign up to one and put my best foot forward into the world of internet dating. I head on in there with my best pictures and witty one-liners, and I don't know what I expect, but I never get it. It's always the same – approaches based solely on their sexual desires, catfishes or weird married men. Occasionally they appear nice, and I get a few dull conversations with a few dull men, but I don't think I've achieved a first date from a dating app in well over a year. I am partly to blame for this, because I fizzle out conversations too. I find it hard to get excited about it all and to showcase my personality without feeling like a massive cringebag. Within about three weeks I get bored/drained/lose all hope in humanity and I delete and vow never to use an app again. Until next time . . .

Single and ready to tingle

At this point I wonder if the only thing I'm missing is sex and I start to convince myself that what I really need is just a bit of intimacy, some male company, some attention and an orgasm. So I initiate 'Hey, stranger' WhatsApp conversations with guys I have dated in the past and sometimes even significant exes – those I'd vowed never to let near my vagina again. I get to the point of arranging to see them, but then I chicken out because I remember that the likelihood of an orgasm is pretty slim and that there is infinitely more chance of one when I'm alone. (In fact, that's quite a powerful anti-fuckboy tool – make yourself cum before you arrange to see them. The desire to see them may well have worn off by the time you're finished. Some people call this pre-bating.) It's hard because in order to have a bit of fun I need to find the man fit, funny and fuckable. I have to like him *and* fancy him. The problem is that if I like him and fancy him, it's highly likely that I will catch feelings at some point, so a potential fuckbuddy sort of has to be hot but not an intellectual match, and I really don't want that again. I have learned from past mistakes that I cannot do casual sex very well and that I often regret it the moment they cum and I haven't. This stage makes me feel that I am attractive and that I do have options. I feel quite empowered when I don't end up sleeping with an ex and so I return to the single and content stage.

It's okay not to feel happy about being single at all times. It is normal to have days, or weeks, where you wallow in how shit and lonely it is. You are allowed to feel jealousy when your colleague announces her pregnancy, you are allowed to think, 'She has the personality of a lasagne – why the fuck is she more successful at finding love than me?' You are allowed to watch IG stories of happy couples and think, 'Oh, bore off, you pair of dickheads.' You are allowed to periodically reinstall Tinder because you feel lonely and then freak out because the only people swiping right for you look like they've just been released from an extremely hard stay in prison. You are allowed to invent a long-distance boyfriend to shut your family up. You are allowed to decline wedding invitations because you feel embarrassed about being the only one who doesn't have a plus one. You are allowed to feel all the feelings and to have regular wobbles. You just have to know how to pull yourself back from that and return to the 'single and content' mindset.

It's a cliché, I know, but the most effective way of becoming at peace with being single is to practise self-love. 'Love' is not only a noun, so it's more than a feeling; it's a verb, so it's also an action. To love yourself means to actively show yourself love, care and nurturing. If you have a pet, you don't just show love through the power of your mind, you love your pet by grooming it, feeding it, giving it affection and, if you're anything like me, singing love songs to it on a regular basis.

> **To love yourself means to care for yourself, and that can come in any form that works for you.**

For me, on days when I manage to exercise, meditate, eat well, take care of my skin and get a good cuddle from my son or my dog, I always feel much more at peace. On days when I am rushed off my feet and I eat crap all day, take off my make-up with a baby wipe, don't manage more than a two-minute dog walk around the block and generally just don't look after myself, I always feel much more fraught when I get into bed at night. I start thinking that this would all be so much easier if I just had a man.

Working on the relationship that we have with ourselves is vital, and it leads to much healthier relationships with others in the future. Sometimes we can do this by going on a journey of self-development: discovering new things, taking up hobbies, volunteering, consuming content that helps us to develop self-love, getting a bit more spiritual, joining single women's groups and filling up our time with self-care activities. Dating yourself is also a really nice thing to do. Buy yourself flowers, get dressed up, take yourself out for dinner or to the cinema, or have a nice take-away and then masturbate.

Sometimes we need a helping hand to unpick some of the stuff that has made us link singledom to unworthiness, or to help us cope with the loneliness or grief associated with not realizing our family's dream for us, or with being childless not by choice. Therapy or counselling is excellent for this if you are able to access it (resources at the back of the book) and, coupled with self-love and care, it should help you to feel more accepting – and even proud – of your single status.

We have to rewire the conditioning that has made us feel that being single means anything other than you just haven't met the person who fits or that you're perfectly content by yourself. We need to normalize

buy
yourself
flowers

take
yourself
out for
dinner

and then
masturbate

or have
a nice
take-away

finding that person at any stage of life and we also need to normalize never finding that person. Relationships are not the be all and end all. We don't all have to aspire to the outdated model of marriage in your early twenties, babies in your late twenties. We can live fun and fulfilled lives and then meet the love of our lives at fifty or sixty. Spending your twenties and thirties in a toxic relationship that you need to recover from is far harder than spending those decades working on your own contentment.

> **We need to stop seeing romantic relationships as the holy grail, because many of them aren't even very romantic, and some are far lonelier to be in than being on your own.**

If you have had relationships in the past, consider some of the bad ones. Would you choose to go back to that over being single? I wouldn't. I would rather be single until the day I die than spend a moment longer with any of those men.

People need human connection and interaction, we need love and care, but that does not have to come from a romantic partner. If you don't have love, then that needs to change, but if your soul is fulfilled by friends, family and self-love, then being single is not an affliction or a jail sentence, it's a choice, and it's equally as worthy a choice as being in a couple. And even if it's not a choice, enjoy being single while it lasts because it won't last for ever (unless you want it to), and there will always be times in your future relationships when you miss your single days. Accept where you are and accept that not having found someone is not a sign that you are not worthy, it's simply a sign that your person hasn't yet crossed your path (they will come, so enjoy your singleness until they get here). Or it's a sign that you're absolutely bossing single life and you don't need a partner to 'complete' you. It's better to be single than settle.

Being single is not an affliction or a jail sentence.

Chapter 3:

Do the work first

I was cheated on in the worst way by my last boyfriend. He slept with a close friend of mine and now they're engaged. I was pretty insecure before due to what some might call 'Daddy issues,' but now my self-esteem is on the floor. My current partner is the first person I have been with since the cheating ex. We've been together for six months and I have told him everything about the past. Our relationship is good, but rocky, which he blames me for. I check his phone often, and I struggle with him going out without me, so whenever he plans to see his friends, we always end up arguing. He says I'm controlling. I feel really hurt by that because it feels like he is dismissing what my ex put me through and how much that impacts on how I feel about myself. I fully admit that I am insecure and that I do need to change, but am I right to think that he should be acknowledging why I am like this and being more sensitive to that?

*W*hy we behave the way we do is a really important thing to figure out, because it helps us to recognize when we are the ones waving the red flags in relationships and how to put them right. We are a product of our environment and experiences, and sometimes that results in us carrying some unhealthy traits into dating and relationships – but it doesn't excuse us from subjecting people to unpleasant behaviour or abuse. People often ask, 'Is there something wrong with me?' to unlock the key as to why they are single or why their relationships keep failing, and if that question relates to looks, body size, interests and hobbies or sexual experience, then the answer will always be a resounding *No*:

> **There is nothing wrong with you – you just haven't met the right person.**

However, the uncomfortable truth is that sometimes we do need to look inside ourselves and reflect on whether there are any patterns in our relationships that we keep repeating, or whether there are any of our own behaviours that we need to address. The harsh reality is that sometimes we are the toxic one. It's not that there is something inherently wrong with us, it's just that we have learned behaviours that do not make for healthy relationships or make people run before we even get to a relationship.

bell hooks writes in *All About Love* (essential reading), 'When we understand that love is the will to nurture our own and another's spiritual growth then we cannot claim to love when we are hurtful and abusive. Love and abuse cannot co-exist.' This applies to self-love too; if we are hurtful and abusive towards ourselves, then we will struggle to give and receive love from others. When we are taught that we are unworthy of love at all, or that we are only lovable under certain conditions (for example, when we are behaving), then this has an impact on our ability to love ourselves. It is much harder to achieve self-love and healthy relationships if we have never truly been shown love or that we are worthy of love. How can we hope to have a healthy relationship with someone else when we don't even have one with ourselves?

Let's take a closer look at the factors that might be influencing our behaviour in romantic settings.

Attachment theory

As a social work student, attachment theory was at the core of my learning. It is a theory that was developed by John Bowlby and Mary Ainsworth in the 1960s to help us understand relationships between children and their caregivers by observing how babies react when they are separated from their caregivers and how these early attachments impact on their coping mechanisms. It has since been developed by other researchers in the fields of psychology and social work to look at how our early attachments influence how we form connections in adult relationships. *Attached* by Amir Levine and Rachel S. F. Heller is a great starting point if you want to learn more.

In early life, we develop coping mechanisms and behaviour strategies from surviving or thriving under certain care-giving styles. Looking at our childhoods and our patterns in adult relationships can help us to identify our attachment style. Figuring out our personal attachment style is the first step in putting down our weapons and learning to use a different set of tools.

Secure attachment

If you were lucky enough to experience a consistently loving and nurturing environment in your childhood, where your needs were met

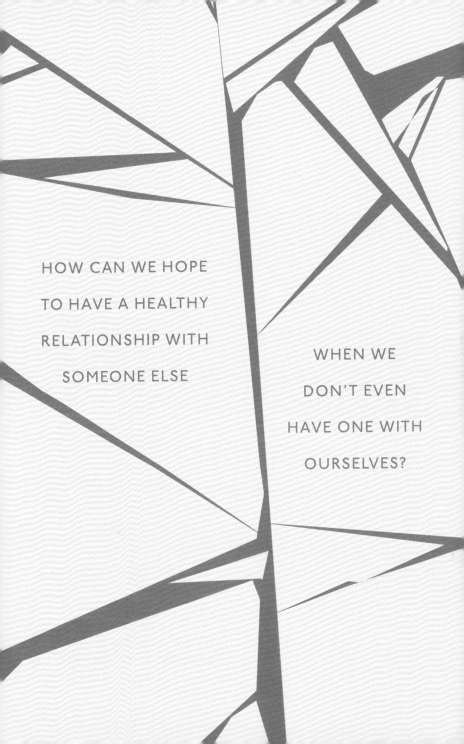

HOW CAN WE HOPE
TO HAVE A HEALTHY
RELATIONSHIP WITH
SOMEONE ELSE

WHEN WE
DON'T EVEN
HAVE ONE WITH
OURSELVES?

and you felt safe in the knowledge that you were valued unconditionally, you are likely to go into adult relationships being open to developing strong emotional bonds. Having a good experience of human interaction in the early days leads people to view themselves and others positively, to have high self-esteem, to feel comfortable with expressing emotions and to feel happy with the mutual exchange of dependence in a relationship. This doesn't mean that all your relationships will be easy, particularly if you date people with insecure attachment styles, but it means that you are more likely to have the skills to deal with relationship problems as you find it easy to communicate your needs and you do not become instantly defensive about criticism. You find it easy to trust people because you have learned that you can rely on others. You are also just as comfortable being single as you are being in a relationship, as you have developed the tools for self-love and self-soothing. If you do experience challenges within your relationship, you are able to express your thoughts and feelings clearly and rationally without allowing them to feel like a reflection of your unworthiness.

Dismissive-avoidant

A dismissive-avoidant attachment style usually develops in people whose parents or carers met their basic care needs but who were emotionally unavailable. For example, your parent might have made sure that you had everything materially, but when you approached them about feeling sad, they minimized your pain and told you to stop being silly. No space was given to hear you out or to tend to things that were unsettling for you. You learned to keep your feelings to yourself, because they didn't matter as long as you had a roof over your head and food in your belly. You were unable to depend on your parents to meet your emotional needs and so you learned that you couldn't depend on others. Adults with a dismissive-avoidant attachment style find it difficult to express their feelings and tend to keep things bottled up, so find it hard to be in intimate relationships. If this is you, you will come across as emotionally unavailable and quite aloof. You won't easily seek therapy, especially because this attachment style gives you a positive view of yourself but a negative view of other people, so it's easy to blame others for the things that go wrong in your relationships. Self-reflection will be minimal and you won't have time for other people's issues. You will minimize their feelings and think that they should just stop moaning and get on with it. You will avoid intimacy because you don't believe that you need it. You may appear confident and self-assured, tend to be independent and self-sufficient and can come across as cold. You will be wary about opening yourself up to relationships and will have a tendency to pull away when things start to get serious. You will prefer casual relationships to committed ones and will freak out and feel suffocated when somebody appears too nice.

I think it's no surprise that many of us will have dated men who fit this type; I believe that this is connected to how we raise boys in early life. When boys fall over and cry, we tend to tell them to 'be brave' and 'man up'. We teach them that crying isn't manly. We give them less space to be vulnerable because we tend to raise them into the strong male protector role. They grow to believe that emotions are a feminine thing and they have to bottle them up in order to be a man. All of this can contribute to developing a dismissive-avoidant attachment style.

Anxious

An anxious attachment style usually develops in people who had inconsistent parenting. For example, a child who has an absent parent or one who shows up only occasionally may develop this attachment style. They love the absent parent, and when that parent does return they give the child attention and shower them with gifts, which makes the child feel loved and wanted. And then they disappear again, until next Christmas. The child inevitably idolizes this parent and then blames themselves for not being enough to keep them around. It makes them want to fight harder for their attention and they come to rely on that parent's inconsistent presence for validation. If you have an anxious attachment style, you may come across as needy, sensitive and clingy in relationships. You will need constant attention and reassurance and will be very sensitive to not feeling loved. You will become quickly infatuated with partners, sometimes to the point of obsession. (Chapter 6 covers limerence, which is heavily connected to this attachment style.) You will be on the lookout for imperceptible changes in their behaviour and will freak if they don't answer your messages for an extended period. You may have a tendency to massively over-analyse small things. You may be comfortable with expressing your feelings, but this may be done in quite an intense way. You will need constant validation and will find it hard to validate yourself, so you seek approval from others. You will probably feel anxious when your partner is not around and will only feel settled when you feel that your partner is interacting positively with you. Rejection and criticism will feel gut-wrenching. It is important to you to feel liked by everyone, but you will often feel that people are taking you for granted or aren't appreciating you. You will find it hard to set boundaries and will often bend over backwards to please people.

Disorganized-fearful

This attachment style is usually found in people who have experienced significant trauma in childhood. When the person who was supposed to keep you safe is someone who you feared, you grow to learn that nobody is safe and that love is scary. If you have this attachment style, you will probably feel that you want to have intimate relationships, but you will be scared of letting people in. You will find it very hard to trust people and will be terrified of rejection. You might question the motives of anyone who tries to get close to you because you don't feel worthy of love. Kindness from partners will make you feel suspicious because you have low self-esteem and do not feel deserving of positive attention; you have been let down by people in the past so have learned that even those who promise to love you can't be trusted. You may find it difficult to manage anger and will find yourself taking it out on those closest to you, or you may become quite submissive and find yourself tolerating anger from partners. You also find it hard to set boundaries.

You may read these summaries and feel that you have traits of several of the styles, and that is normal. Attachment occurs on a spectrum, ranging from the extreme end to the less extreme. We can experience different parenting styles from different caregivers so we can end up moving between different styles. Our adult relationships can also influence us to change our attachment style.

> **The good news is that our attachment style is not permanent – we can rewire it.**

Again, therapy is extremely helpful for this. For example, therapy can help a dismissive-avoidant person learn how to explore sharing their feelings and how to work on empathy, or help an anxious person learn how to set boundaries.

Co-dependency

Co-dependency is a circular relationship in which one person needs another person who in turn needs to be needed. The co-dependent person, known as 'the giver', feels worthless unless they are needed by – and making sacrifices for – the enabler, otherwise known as 'the taker.' According to co-dependency coach Jo Westwood (@jowestwood on Instagram), co-dependency is a feminist issue because much of it stems from being automatically assigned a care-giving role in which you are expected to nurture and look after your loved ones but not to receive anything in return. Co-dependency is a deep-rooted coping mechanism that usually develops at a young age as a response to some level of dysfunction happening in your home life. The definition of co-dependency that Jo offers is that it's 'an addiction to external validation and to dysfunctional, often one-way relationships'. It can be triggered by any number of big or small traumas, including but not limited to being brought up in a high-conflict home; having a narcissistic and/or co-dependent parent (often one of each); sexual, physical or verbal abuse, either witnessed or experienced; an emotionally or physically absent parent; and divorce or addiction in the family home. Jo explains that a common thread between people who become co-dependent is that there is a strong sense in their early years set-up that there's a price of admission to pay to be part of the gang. It often includes taking care of people who should be taking care of you, making excuses for their behaviour, keeping their secrets and telling lies to protect them. If you don't play that game, you betray your family system and put your child-self at risk of being abandoned and neglected.

So how might co-dependency manifest in adult relationships?

- **A low sense of self-worth, which means you often settle for the bare minimum in relationships**
- **Hypervigilance, which you think is intuition**
- **A chronic need to please those around you, even/especially those who treat you badly, resulting in over-giving your time, energy and money**
- **Deriving your sense of worth from doing rather than being**
- **An inability to identify or express your own feelings without first knowing what someone else thinks or feels about a situation**

- **Difficulty setting and even more difficulty maintaining boundaries**
- **Confusion or numbness around your own identity. You struggle to know who you are if you're not directly relating to someone else.**

Jo states that co-dependents accept and allow unacceptable behaviour into all areas of their lives. 'You'll probably find yourself stuck in a cycle of dysfunctional and draining one-way relationships (you're always giving, they're always taking), possibly suffering varying forms and levels of neglect and abuse and using manipulation techniques to get the most basic of needs met, yet feeling too confused, drained and down on yourself to lift yourself out of it.'

Co-dependent people and narcissistic people often gravitate towards each other because they fit each other's needs. The narcissist wants constant adoration and the co-dependent person wants to please and adore. The co-dependent person is happy for their needs to play second fiddle to the narcissist's. It suits them to place the narcissist first because it means that they don't have to focus on themselves. Jo says that healing co-dependency does not lie in trying to change your partner/parent/boss (you've been trying that for years already; it hasn't worked!). The key is bringing your focus back to you, building your sense of self-worth, discovering your own identity and learning to do the hard thing and express your wants and needs clearly. Until you can do that, you continue to play your part in perpetuating the cycle. Contacting a co-dependency coach like Jo can help you to begin to make changes. Therapy can also help, as can contacting Co-dependents Anonymous (codauk.org). Yup – co-dependency is so addictive that there are AA-style fellowships to help you address it. You may also wish to understand more about sex and love addiction. The Priory Group describes sex and love addiction as

not measured or diagnosed in quantity but instead by the negative impact and consequences associated with the behaviour, on yourself and others. It is characterized by obsessive feelings and behaviours which the sufferer feels compelled to repeat regardless of the consequences. These behaviours and thoughts get progressively worse, ultimately resulting in the breakdown of personal relationships. This repetitive pattern with negative consequences can happen both as a result of excessive acting out (sexual bulimia) or the opposite (sexual anorexia).

The characteristics associated with this type of behaviour are listed on the Sex and Love Addicts Anonymous (SLAA) website. Check to see if you meet the characteristics and seek support if you feel you need it.

Mental health

I have focused on attachment styles and co-dependency above. It would take an entire book to write about every psychological issue that exists and how each one might impact on our love lives as a whole. But I do think we need to take a quick look at how mental health might also have an impact. Here's what clinical psychologist Dr Mayowa Aina (@dr.mayus on Instagram) has to say around the impact of mental health on dating.

Regardless of your mental health status, or whether or not you have been diagnosed, it is important to pay attention to your attachment style, as this is likely to have the biggest impact on how you respond and react in relationships. Finding a partner with an attachment style that works well with yours is key. Somebody with an anxious attachment style might be compatible with a person who is securely attached; two people with anxious attachments might work well together. The thing to remember is that if either you or your partner has a dismissive-avoidant attachment style, then this may be a big barrier to having a relationship that meets your needs and so work needs to be done.

However, Dr Aina states that it is still essential that we understand how our mental health might also have an impact on dating and how to stop this negatively affecting our partners. Mental health problems present differently in different people. For example, people with anxiety might experience hypersensitivity around perceived behaviour changes in their partner. Some may respond by running away and distancing themselves from their lover, while others may overcompensate and become very intense for fear of losing their partner. Only you will know how your mental health impacts on you, but it is important that we don't end up hurting others and using our mental health as a justification.

For example, depression may leave you feeling as though you cannot get out of bed or face communicating with anyone, but it is not kind to ignore a partner or someone you are regularly dating for days on end, leaving them feeling anxious and worrying about whether they have been ghosted. Dr Aina says that having an awareness of how your mental health might affect how you show up in relationships means that you can communicate this to partners in advance. So, explaining to a new partner that sometimes you suffer periods of depression that make communicating very difficult for you, and letting them know that if there are some days when you are less responsive it may be because of this, can help you both have a healthier relationship. We owe partners information about how our mental health might impact on them; it gives them the ability to choose whether they are the right person to cope with that and it also allows them not to take it personally if your mental health affects how you treat them. However, I would wait to drop in the mental health and attachment issues talk until you know you like them. It's not first-date conversation, not least because it makes you vulnerable to those who may wish to take advantage of people who appear more fragile.

Whatever our diagnosis may be, it is worth making sure that we don't allow the symptoms or outcomes that we experience as a result of our mental health to become an excuse to be abusive to our partners. We still owe them communication, courtesy and respect. You are not your anxiety, you are not your depression, you are not your personality disorder; you are a whole and complete person with a complex personality who also happens to experience mental health issues that can have an impact on how you relate to and interact with others. You have the right to set boundaries and you have the right to focus on your own mental health when necessary, but you do not have the right to have a negative impact on someone else's mental health by failing to communicate properly or failing to respect their boundaries.

Past hurt

Like the woman quoted at the start of this chapter, we can end up learning to behave in toxic ways as a result of our previous relationships. It stands to reason that being cheated on has a huge impact on the way we feel about ourselves and on the way we might approach relationships in the future. To be betrayed by someone you trusted is earth-shattering, especially if your attachment style, low self-confidence or anxiety disorder made it hard to trust them in the first place. The same goes for abuse of any kind – at its most basic level, it's a betrayal of your trust. Experiencing abuse or cheating can also alter your attachment style. It can make you extremely cautious about future partners and cause you to act in ways that you may feel are protecting you from being hurt again but which are hurting your new partner.

> **If you are checking your partner's phone and causing arguments to prevent them going out, then you have become toxic.**

You might have a good reason to justify why you are so worried about cheating, but that does not excuse you from controlling or hurting your current partner.

If past relationships have led you to becoming the toxic one, then use your understanding of how you got here as the starting point for your healing, but don't use it as an excuse to remain stuck.

Being cautious after trauma is important and rebuilding your ability to trust again before getting back into dating is essential. What we mustn't do is enter into things before we are ready and punish our new partner for the sins of the old one. And if we decide to stay with the old sinner, then we mustn't use the sin as a weapon – if you stay with them after finding evidence of cheating, then you need to do so on the basis that you are going to work through it and come out stronger as a couple, not use it as a stick to beat them with for ever. If their previous betrayal means that you are wildly accusing your beau of cheating or controlling who they speak to or where they go, or expecting them to bend over backwards constantly to reassure you of their innocence, or not letting your emotional guard down and developing an insecure attachment style, then you need to reconsider if it's healthy for you to remain in the relationship. If you're single but still carrying the burden of the damage caused to you by previous cheating, then you need to do the work before you are ready to start dating again. Imagine embarking on a relationship with a man who doesn't trust women. He might well have good reason, he might have been fucked over by every woman he has trusted, but if he approaches your relationship from a position of being wary of all women and expects you to jump through hoops to prove that you are not like other women, then your relationship is going to be tainted from the start.

Sweet but a psycho

An interesting phenomenon on social media is the abundance of memes that poke fun at the stereotype of the crazy girlfriend. Memes like 'When he hasn't texted you back after ten minutes so you slash his tyres' or tweets like 'Good pussy and psychotic behaviour go hand in hand, you can't have one without the other' regularly do the rounds on socials. Women in the comments will be gleefully tagging one another in recognition. We have to recognize the influence of these tropes and how they seep into our consciousness. It would be shocking for a man to make a meme that says that he would stab his girlfriend if she didn't text him back after five minutes, yet we laugh when it's the other way around.

Just like memes that normalize rape culture, normalizing 'psycho' behaviour from women as hilarious really does us a disservice. Since time began, men have been calling us crazy (look up how the word 'hysteria' came about) in response to us expressing our emotions. It is used to belittle our very valid emotional reactions to things or to gaslight us into thinking that the only reason we are concerned about a man we're involved with texting his ex at 3 a.m. is because we are psychotic. It is used by men to silence and discredit us.

When a man claims that all of his exes are crazy it should be seen as a red flag, because it usually indicates that he has driven them to the point of madness, that he has dismissed their rational emotional responses to his behaviour, or that he is covering his tracks in case such an ex contacts you to warn you about him. I'm all for reclaiming words that have been used against us, but I don't think that 'psycho'/'crazy'/'insane' should be included in this, not least because they are ableist, but also because they are still very much used as a way to shut women up or to belittle our emotions.

> Buying into the whole 'I put the hot in psychotic' narrative simply allows men to continue to dismiss our valid feelings.

And if you are the type to genuinely act in ways that might meet the criteria for 'crazy', then that really is not a characteristic you should be proudly hanging on to. It is a big sign that you need professional help.

Being 'sweet but a psycho' is clearly going to be harmful to partners and we should not subscribe to it just because Instagram makes it seem acceptable.

We should also acknowledge how much the whole 'psycho' trope is linked to our emotions or to changes in mood caused by the hormones of people who have periods. How would cisgender men feel if they had blood pouring out of their bum holes for three to seven days (sometimes longer) twelve times a year (sometimes more) and they were just expected to carry on as normal while either wearing a small nappy or shoving a cotton stick or cup up there? They would freak the fuck out. I don't think they would even go to work; if it were cis men who menstruated, there would probably be 'period days' when they were all legally entitled to take time off work every time they came on. In fact, they would probably have pumped so much money into research about periods they'd have found some way to make it a delightful experience. We have so much to contend with – the bloating, the debilitating pain, the spots, the gaining half a stone, the monumental hormone changes that affect the way we see, feel, taste, react and respond to everything. Our sleep is affected, so we often feel fatigued, emotional and irrational; we feel the effects before it even arrives. And then there are those with endometriosis, polycystic ovary syndrome, menopause symptoms, or no periods at all. And don't even get me started on birth control. Periods – or lack of periods – can become a major, life-changing thing. So we must rebuke people when they accuse us of being 'crazy' when we cry at something, like an advert, and they think it's irrational, or when they call us a psycho for being sensitive, or criticize us for being indecisive. We are trying to handle life while bleeding out of our genitalia in order to ensure the survival of the human race and we should rate ourselves highly for that. Men need to educate themselves on just how big an effect periods and birth control can have on people who bleed and learn to understand how they can help to make it easier. We are dealing with shit that most cis men couldn't handle even on their best days. They need to show some respect.

We're perfectly sane and it's perfectly rational for our emotional state to change throughout the month.

Fuckgirls

We can be fuckgirls too. I feel that it's slightly different because men haven't been systemically and systematically oppressed by women since time began, and because there is definitely a sense that it's less likely that a man is going to feel like he was used for sex by a woman and, in most cases, if he was, he'd probably just be happy that he got to have sex. He is not at risk of being shamed for it, and there is a high chance he would have got an orgasm out of it. It's just different. But there are certainly ways in which we use men that are somewhat equivalent to the ways in which they use us.

There is a small brand of feminism that promotes seeing men as cash cows and using them for money. It suggests allowing men you *know* you don't like to take you out so you can use them for a free dinner and thinking less of men who don't fund our lives or lavish us with gifts. (This is not the same as expecting a man to pay on the first date.) It's a brand of 'get the bag' feminism and it promotes dating for money rather than for love. I understand the mentality, I really do. The gender pay gap is real – men are able to earn significantly more than us, and they don't have to have enforced career breaks when they have children. I would be absolutely thrilled to meet a multimillionaire who decided that he wanted to spend his money on me, but, as the mother of a son, I would be horrified to think that if he grows up to be wealthy some women will see him as nothing more than an opportunity to get rich.

WE ARE DEALING WITH SHIT THAT MOST CIS MEN COULDN'T HANDLE EVEN ON THEIR BEST DAYS.

THEY NEED TO SHOW SOME RESPECT.

> **If greed and the pursuit of money is the driving factor in your interpersonal relationships, then you will never know love.**

In *All About Love* bell hooks writes of the time when she interviewed Lil' Kim: 'The culture of greed validates and legitimises her worship of money, it is not at all interested in her emotional growth. Who cares if she ever knows love? Sadly, like so many Americans, she believes that the pursuit and attainment of wealth will compensate for all emotional lack.' But we know that it doesn't. Being rich does not make you emotionally fulfilled; it just means you can hate yourself in luxurious surroundings.

Dating men who *want* to spend money on you is fine – when both parties are on board with the arrangement. But to use men for money is not only harmful to them because you have created a relationship under false pretences, it is harmful to us too. It means that we deny ourselves the ability to experience true love and emotional connections; it means that we only ever experience transactional relationships. And it also makes us much more vulnerable to abuse. Being financially dependent on a man is a huge barrier to leaving toxic or abusive relationships. It also gives some men the idea that they own you or that you owe them something. Often, there will be an expectation that you will have sex whenever and however they want because, essentially, they believe they've paid for it. I don't believe that there is anything liberating or empowering about using men for money. In fact, it's quite the opposite. Being financially reliant on men is utterly disempowering. (Using men for necessity to survive, or sex work, is not included in this.)

I recently had a poll question on my Instagram where a woman asked whether it was bad that she had lied to the guy she was sleeping with about being on contraception. The fact that this is even a question is worrying. I would hope that most women wouldn't want to intentionally dupe a man into pregnancy for any reason, regardless of whether that's to keep him or just because you want a baby, but let me make it very clear:

It is a vile and evil thing to remove someone's agency and ability to choose.

It's not only cruel to him but, really, you are harming yourself. Parenting is hard, and purposely choosing to do it in a deceptive way, which is more likely to make the guy run than stay, is not likely to end well for anyone. Aside from this deception, if you haven't had children yet it is worth remembering the importance of choosing the right relationships to potentially have children within. While we can absolutely boss it as single parents, most will tell you that it's a two-person job and that having children with the wrong person makes that job even harder. Having children to 'keep' somebody or because you think it will improve an already failing relationship is a terrible idea. It is still the case that, in most heterosexual couples, the woman will do the lion's share of childcare. Women's lives change beyond recognition after having children, while men's often barely change at all.

His life will remain much the same: he won't have to alter his working hours, he can go out, live spontaneously, while you're stuck at home struggling to find time to poo, let alone to get your hair done. You will find it harder to date because you can never be spontaneous again. Obviously, it's not all doom and gloom; once it happens, you make it work, eventually you find your rhythm and you can rebuild and do brilliantly well, but your life will never be your own again, and you've really got to think about how heavy the burden is on mothers before you ever consider allowing any sperm near your un-contracepted vagina. Is it worth altering your entire life for this man? Being the centre of attention at an Insta-worthy baby shower looks cute, but that's the easy part: making the commitment to bring another human into the world is a huge thing and we need to treat it as such.

*

Being financially dependent on a man is a huge barrier to leaving toxic or abusive relationship.

Another way in which we often become fuckgirls is when we take advantage of nice men we are not interested in. Putting someone in the friend zone if you're not into them is fine, but if you know that he has feelings for you and you exploit those, then that's cruel. I saw a post on Instagram where a guy was wishing his best friend happy birthday. The caption was full of praise for her and how wonderful she was and it ended with him writing, 'I know that you'll be drunk texting me after your party tonight asking me to come get you at 1 a.m., and you know I'll be there to keep you safe, as always.' My heart really broke for him – *she didn't even invite you to her birthday party, bro!*

I have been in this situation before, and I definitely behaved like a complete bitch. I knew that this man was in love with me, I knew that I would never be interested in him, but I also found it quite handy to have someone around who was willing to do literally anything for me. I took advantage of his feelings by giving him a false sense that maybe one day I might consider a relationship with him. If I had been clear that I absolutely was not and never would be interested, then it would have been up to him if he wanted to be that friend who bends over backwards, but he was doing that in the hope that it would make me love him, and I knew that but I let him continue until I reflected on it and realized how nasty I was being. We are no longer friends.

Unfuck yourself

If you've read this chapter and found it relatable, that might be a sign that you need to start working on yourself before you next download Hinge. So, how do we do the work?

Obviously, therapy and counselling are the first port of call.

Therapy comes in many different forms. Have a look at the NHS website listed at the back of the book to see what style of therapy might be best for you. There is also a list of resources for affordable therapy there. Read the books, write a journal, watch YouTube videos by qualified experts. Attend to your mental health if you're finding it hard to manage. Get professional support. You are entitled to it, and it is in no way embarrassing or means that you are weak. While you are waiting for therapy, you can start by figuring out your attachment style – there is a wealth of online resources to help you; just make sure you access information from legitimate sources. Speak to friends, talk about what you are trying to do, seek help, ask people for therapy recommendations.

Be open to a new mindset and a new way of life.

Commit to sorting your shit out. Writer Yung Pueblo encourages us to 'Find a partner who realizes how their emotional history impacts the way they show up in your relationship. They don't need to know themselves perfectly or have healed all of their old hurt, they just need enough self-awareness to see when their past is getting in the way of loving you right.' Commit to being that partner. Commit to doing something about it.

The bottom line is that all of us are a little bit damaged. Figuring out whether this stems from childhood, previous relationships or is a result of a mental health disorder (or a combination of them all) is essential in helping us to start to heal. There is no shame in any of it, and we should forgive ourselves for the ways in which our unhealed selves might have acted in the past. Reflecting on the shit that we have brought to relationships and trying to unravel it can be hard, but unless we do it we will keep repeating the same patterns and sabotaging our own happiness. Once you have that self-awareness and you do the work, you will be in prime mode to face whatever fuckboy the universe decides to throw at you.

Chapter 4:

Not all men, but definitely these men

Trigger warning: Domestic abuse

I took myself out of the dating game for five years. I was tired and I'd had enough, but I have worked on myself and healed from my past heartbreak, and now I am ready to put myself out there and meet someone new. However, I am worried that I will miss red flags because I'm out of practice and a bit rusty. Is there any sure-fire way of spotting fuckboys before becoming attached to them?

A fuckboy is a man who hurts, uses, controls, manipulates, deceives or just generally and knowingly brings misery or stress to the women with whom he is romantically involved. The term is slightly misleading, as it makes it sound like it's only young guys who do this, but fuckboys exist at any age – fuckgrandads are a thing, but we'll stick with 'fuckboy', as it's a well-recognized term. Fuckboy fuckbuggery is, sadly, rife in twenty-first-century dating. Most of us have encountered a fuckboy at some point, so it's important for us to have tools to identify them quickly. This guide is to help you spot them and to understand the red flags before you end up dating them.

A quick note before we get started: these categories are not exclusive. A fuckboy can fall into more than one grouping. You might encounter a no-labels narcissistic roadman fuckboy or an abusive wasteman spiritual fuckboy.

It's bad enough if they fit firmly into one category, but if they straddle several you need to run for your life.

Fuckgirls and fucknon-binaries exist too. The types explored here could each be women or non-binary people, so apply these stereotypes to whoever you date.

To be clear, I am specifically talking about fuckboys here. Not all feminist, spiritiual or privileged men are fuckboys; what makes these guys bad is that they use their feminism, spirituality or privilege to fuck women over.

Feminist fuckboy

There are two types of feminist fuckboy. There's the type who knows he is not a feminist by any stretch of the imagination but pretends to be one because he knows that doing so makes it much easier to manipulate women into trusting him. He is a wokefish, but he can't keep up the façade for long before he is compelled to come out with some 'Not all men . . .' nonsense. Then there's the type who genuinely thinks that he is a feminist; he wholeheartedly believes in equality but he also believes that his feminism entitles him to respect from women. Deep down, he feels that we owe him something for defending our corner; he thinks that he is special and should be treated as such. And it can be easy to fall into the trap of handing out medals to nice men for simply being nice because the bar is set so fucking low.

It is hard to spot fake feminist fuckboys because they know exactly what they are supposed to say. They will have read the right books and will post the right posts, they'll be a paid-up member of the Labour or Green party and Lizzo and Cardi B will be among their favourite artists because they make them feel empowered. The fake feminist fuckboy will play the acoustic guitar and you will melt when he bashfully strums you a song that he wrote called 'Solidarit-HE' which details his own personal route into feminism and all the backlash *he* has suffered from men on *his* journey. It's not until the moment he lays down his guitar and asks for a blow job then gets pissed off when you refuse that it becomes clear it was all a smokescreen.

There are some tell-tale signs to look out for – for example, if he talks about it too much. Genuine male feminists just *are*, it's just part of their psyche; they acknowledge their privilege and the times when they have misused it. They have a clear understanding of consent and they genuinely respect women. They understand the importance of empowering women and how that benefits society as a whole, and they don't go on about it all the time. Feminist fuckboys will make it part of their identity; they will want to talk about it with every woman they meet, and they will expect praise in return. But a real feminist would be wanting to discuss this with the men they meet instead. Feminist fuckboys want to be applauded for their feminism and they feel a little miffed if they don't get the recognition they feel they deserve. They will also mansplain to women about women's issues: men in my inbox regularly tell me they are male allies and explain to me the ways in which women feel unsafe. The feminist fuckboy will be the type to tell you that they hate the pressure caused by beauty standards that exist for women before telling you that you shouldn't wear make-up because they prefer 'natural' women.

A great way of figuring out the truth is to look at who he associates with. Are his friends on the same page, or does he hang out with some questionable guys?

> **If he is the only feminist among a bunch of very laddish lads who banter about women they have fucked, then that is very telling.**

Does he pull up those friends when they cross the line? How does he view, and speak about, sex workers or people from marginalized genders, trans women, older women or women he doesn't fancy? He cannot claim to be a feminist if his feminism is not intersectional. Does he acknowledge the importance of equality when it comes to contraception or does he automatically expect you to be the one preventing pregnancy? Does he pull his weight at home or does the burden of domestic tasks fall to you? Fake feminist fuckboys often protest far too much, but they don't back up their claims with consistent decent behaviour towards women. If he wrote the lyrics to his song 'Solidarit-HE' while sitting in a café but he didn't tip the waitress who served him, he's definitely a fake.

Narcissistic fuckboy

If you have experienced abuse in a relationship, that does not mean that the perpetrator is a narcissist, despite what social media tells you.

Of course some of them are, but the vast majority of abusers are not. Narcissism is defined by a specific set of behaviours that occur consistently. You can be selfish, violent, controlling and lack empathy without being a narcissist. In cases where the abuse victim is a woman, those behaviours very often stem from the person being a misogynist, not a narcissist. I say this because everyone on social media seems to associate all domestic violence with narcissism, and that is simply not the case. However, relationships with narcissistic people are often abusive so it's important to be able to identify them.

There are two types of narcissist – covert (think incels, 'woe is me' types, people who blame the world for their lack of success) and overt (think Donald Trump – arrogant, grandiose). A narc typically has an overinflated ego: they are obsessed with how they look and how others see them; they need to be admired. They need to feel important. They have no interest in empathy or how anyone feels but, unlike psychopaths and sociopaths, they are able to experience it. They are manipulative and take advantage of others for their own gain. They are entitled and selfish and will belittle and demean others in order to feel above them. They display over-inflated egos and arrogant self-love to deflect from the fact that, inside, they are deeply damaged and insecure.

Your typical narcissistic fuckboy will be a regular gym user and he will frequently post his workouts on Instagram and Snapchat, because if nobody can see his workout, it didn't count. He will post his protein shakes and meal prep too, because he thinks that everyone is fascinated by what he's going to eat over the next three days. He will often have tattoos and veneers that he had done in Turkey, a nice car and a flashy watch, and he will try to stay on trend. He won't be able to buy a pair of Balenciagas without posting pictures of his purchase on every social media

platform he can think of. You will often see pictures of lions or wolves on his Instagram with captions that suggest that he thinks that he has a lot in common with lions and wolves.

Many narcs promote a lavish lifestyle and some genuinely do live it. Many of the super-wealthy guys you meet will have strong narcissistic tendencies and their Instagram will be full of pictures of cars, yachts and exclusive holidays and motivational quotes about making money. The narc will be very charming and everyone around him will love him. He will be the loudest guy at the bar who buys everyone a round and will turn up to your date in a Porsche. But if he pays for the dinner, you might get a text afterwards asking you to transfer your half as he didn't get anything sexual in return.

Or he might be a covert narcissist, who is not flashy at all, the type who hates those flashy guys and blames them and other successful people for his failings. He may think he is above anyone who watches *Love Island* and look down on people who he feels don't match his intellectual prowess. He feels that the world owes him something and that he is entitled and above others because of his inherent greatness. He will scoff when you tell him that you haven't read Dostoyevsky, and he will belittle you for your book, film or music choices. He will make you feel like a silly child. However, when he finally does approve of something you say or of your movie choice, you will feel validated. He will make you feel like he sets the bar when it comes to intelligence and you will find yourself wanting to prove that you can match that.

The narcissist fuckboy will dominate conversations and it might be hard to get a word in edgeways. When he does stop talking about himself long enough for you to have an input, he will never respond in the right way. He will either dismiss your words or try to use them to criticize you.

For example, if you tell him you've had a disagreement with a friend, instead of listening and supporting you, he'll brush it off as being minor and say something accusatory like 'Why are you always falling out with people? What's wrong with you?'

Narcissists like to turn your emotional reactions back on you. This is a form of gaslighting.

If you say to him, 'I feel like that's not very supportive,' he will start an argument, usually something like 'Oh, so now *I'm* not supportive, after I just paid your gas bill and drove you to work? Okay then.' With most things you raise, they will disagree or know better. You could be a nurse and he could be a plumber, but a narcissistic fuckboy will think he knows more about nursing than you do. A narcissistic fuckboy will often use negging (using back-handed compliments or outright insults intentionally to destroy self-esteem) as a technique to hurt you: he will tell you that you've put on weight or that he's just noticed you have quite a big nose, but he'll say it in a jokey way so that if you get upset he can turn it around on you and accuse you of being oversensitive – this is another example of gaslighting.

Narcissists do not like to be criticized, but they love to dish out criticism.

They want to feel superior to everyone else so they will try to subtly bash your confidence so that you end up feeling inferior to them.

The worst thing about narcissists is that they can be the most unbelievably attentive, loving, caring, charming people you will ever meet. When they want you, which is only when they need you to fulfil some kind of need in them (company, intimacy, sex, an ego boost, somewhere to stay), they will treat you like the sexiest, most important woman in the world. That's what gets you hooked.

When they're good, they're very, very good, but when they are bad, they are terrible. Narcissistic behaviour is very often emotionally abusive. Narcissistic fuckboys will leave you confused, unsure of yourself, constantly questioning whether you are the cause of all the problems – and because they are so charming to everyone else, it can be near impossible to get support around how they are making you feel because everyone around you sees only their wonderful side. Once they have lost interest in you, they will just drop you out. They are often ghosters; they have no consideration whatsoever for how disappearing might affect you and they don't really care. They lack the empathy to be able to understand how their actions affect you, but they also enjoy having the power to negatively affect you. Screaming at a narcissist that he is ruining your life and breaking your heart will be a huge ego boost for him, so don't send emotional paragraphs to tug at their heartstrings; it will only serve to let them know that they have you where they want you.

Narcissists will always stay in touch, at least once a year, usually on birthdays or significant events. They like to keep people interested in them, even if they have no intention of ever making it work with them. They cannot stand the thought of someone not wanting them – even when they don't want that person at all. Narcissists will leave you drained of self-worth. They make you constantly question yourself and they can turn a strong and vocal woman into someone who keeps quiet because it's not worth saying anything at all. These ones are a complete headfuck, and you will lose your sense of yourself if you stay with them for too long. Get rid of them before they drop you in favour of someone they consider to be more of a trophy.

Spiritual fuckboy

The spiritual fuckboy has demonic ways that are hard to spot. His constant declarations of wokeness and enlightenment can fool you into thinking that he's karmically allergic to mistreating another human, but, alas, he is well versed in treating people badly. He just never takes responsibility for it – because the universe made him do it. The first date is likely to involve him inviting you to a yoga class or round to his house to show you his vision board so that he can teach you how to make your own. The spiritual fuckboy is always trying to teach you something, to leave you feeling in awe of him, indebted to him or inferior to him. He might claim that he has magical healing hands, convincing you that he can spiritually cleanse you or bring you closer to the light through the power of touch alone.

> **He offers you reiki but, really, he just wants to finger you.**

You'll find him wearing wooden beaded necklaces and jewellery made from lava stone tied together with cucumber seeds. He may well have mystical-looking tattoos. He's either a heavy weed smoker who takes regular psychedelic trips or he's clean-living and super-conscious about what he puts in his body. He schools you on the damage having a coffee or taking a paracetamol does to your body and to the planet. He's relaxed about unprotected sex, though. He says he doesn't need to worry because he eats seventy-five avocados a day to protect him from venereal disease.

The spiritual fuckboy's dating profile has pictures of his yoga poses or of him seductively sucking mangos while barefoot and topless in Peru. His bio says something like 'vegan, ethereal nemophilist (if you know what that means and you are also a nemophilist, then this is a match made in nirvana)'. He either has no social media at all, not wishing to be a sheep for the masters of deceit who impede our spiritual awakening with constant TikTok dance routines, or he is extremely active on it, using Instagram to broadcast his views on the dangers of social media and how we are being controlled by the BBC. Apart from a couple of shots of him stroking elephants in Kenya with a caption about how humans are wrecking the planet which he wrote in the departure lounge after his seventh long-haul flight of the year, the spiritual fuckboy doesn't post many pictures of himself. He doesn't feel that his physical self is a representation of who he is. He favours quote pictures about the universe and how the earth's centre is akin to a womb.

Your first date with the spiritual fuckboy is amazing. He explains that you have a calming aura while looking suggestively into your eyes. He mentions how humble he is, that he's 'not like other guys', as though they are beneath him, having not yet reached his astounding levels of enlightenment. He labels himself as a humanist, not a feminist, but he extols the virtues of women, discussing at length his views on divine femininity.

To illustrate his deep love for women, he shows you inanimate objects he finds in the park that resemble wombs and vaginas. Or he offers to craft you a sanitary towel out of aloe vera leaves to demonstrate his awe of menstruation. He claims to be the type of man that worships at the altar of the vagina while mansplaining his knowledge of what it means to be a woman. He likes to talk about where women are going wrong, using examples from the animal kingdom to demonstrate the vital importance of women remaining submissive in order for humanity to thrive.

Under this umbrella also comes the religious fuckboy. He uses religion to justify his supposed superiority over women. He is the type who is anti-abortion but will be the first on the phone to the clinic when his mistress gets pregnant. The type to seduce you into casual sex and then tell you that he can't respect a woman who has sex before marriage. Slut-shaming and restrictive gender norms will be his jam. He will use religious holidays as an excuse not to see you, claiming that he is observing the holy day intensely, but two hours later he'll post a Snapchat of him smoking a spliff with his mates. He will class your misdemeanours as sins and will hold them against you, but his misdemeanours will be easily forgiven by God and, obviously, because God has forgiven him, you will have to also.

The spiritual fuckboy is usually a narcissist. He believes his way of thinking to be more sophisticated than yours. Raise an issue with him and he will turn it back on to you and your 'bad energy'. He goes quiet on you for days without explanation. If you have the audacity to mention your discomfort with this, he says he 'took time out to heal'. If you complain, you are accused of interrupting his spiritual evolution. The same 'wokeness' he used to entice you, he now uses to belittle you.

> **He reels you in with his healing vibes and, before you know it, you're in downward dog while he's smashing your chakras out of alignment.**

Eventually, he will fail to contact you because – he'll claim – the mercury in Ur-anus has drained his light-worker vibes.

Criminal fuckboy

(I have used the terminology 'roadman' here as it is a widely recognized, colloquial term that is used to describe active career criminals by the women and girls who are involved with these men. However, unfortunately the term has also been misused in racist ways by being assigned to groups of Black boys who have no involvement in criminality. It should be noted that there are roadmen from every race, religion and community.)

There are several levels of roadmannery and criminality. The low-level roadman is a street dealer who sells drugs directly to users or engages in theft, robbery and gang-related activity. The low-level criminal fuckboy can be identified by his Stone Island puffa jacket, worn fully zipped, with the hood up, regardless of the weather. He has a Nike or Gucci man-bag slung horizontally across his body. He cycles everywhere. His trousers may be worn puzzlingly low, exposing most of his buttocks and grey-looking boxers, as if he wants people to be excited about his bum cheeks. Which is weird, because the roadman fuckboy is notoriously homophobic (unless in relation to encouraging women to have threesomes). This guy has two phones, one being a pay-as-you-go that never stops ringing. Low-level roadman fuckboy smells of Lynx, weed and danger.

LOW-LEVEL ROADMAN FUCKBOY SMELLS OF LYNX, WEED AND DANGER

The mid-level roadman may sell drugs on to the low-level roadman, or he may be running 'deets' (credit-card fraud) or slightly more organized robberies, of other criminals or companies. This roadman is usually flashy. He favours Louboutin trainers and dubiously obtained Rolex watches. He sometimes takes pictures of himself holding wads of money to his ears, as if he is using a phone, like a five-year-old. His Instagram has pictures of his holidays to Miami, Vegas and Dubai (usually paid for with stolen credit cards). He has 'Forex trader' in his Instagram bio. He's got decent money coming in, but he lacks the knowledge and wisdom to do anything sensible with it. He can buy you Balenciaga or rent a penthouse for a month, but he can't offer any security. He's never going to be able to go halves on a mortgage or have any long-term financial stability. His money, like him, is easy come, easy go.

The top-level roadman is more subtle; unlike low-level and mid-level roadman, he doesn't want everyone to know the money he has got coming in. He's smart enough to not risk losing it for the sake of impressing people. He probably graduated from roadman to dodgy businessman a while ago. He might have invested his money into legitimate businesses (garages and take-aways are popular) in order to clean his cash. He owns property and drives a Range Rover. There is normally a long-term partner somewhere, a childhood sweetheart who knows the ins and outs of his operations. He will never leave her and she overlooks his other women in return for a very comfortable lifestyle. The top-level roadman is generally a bit older, sexy, charismatic and filthy in bed.

The thing about all roadmen is that you are never their first priority. He chooses 'doing road' over doing you most of the time. He may even live by the delightful motto 'Money over bitches'. Roadman fuckboys put you at risk. You can become the target of violent repercussions – a lot of gang members are now harming the girlfriends or female relatives of their enemies in retaliation. You can get caught in the crossfire of all sorts of madness just by walking down the road with him. Your house can be raided by the police. Roadman fuckboys often use women to store drugs, money or weapons. If you've been naive enough or forced to look after things for him, you can end up facing criminal charges.

He will probably be in and out of jail, but his sentences will offer some relief because that will be the only time you know for certain where he is.

Dating a roadman is not fun.

He won't be in touch for days because he's got to lie low. He doesn't tend to keep phones for any great length of time, so there's often no way of communicating with him. He deals with nasty, fucked-up people and situations daily. He is damaged and finds it hard to trust you. Post-traumatic stress disorder is common among career criminals. Domestic violence is routine in roadman relationships, as they are often angry and traumatized and encounter violence or threats of violence all day. It's rare for them to not bring that home.

I'm not going to pretend that I don't understand the appeal of roadmen and bad boys in general; believe me, I do. But there comes a point when you really do have to fix up and stop being a dickhead. Prioritize your safety and shatter the rose-tinted Prada glasses. This is a life of police raids, jail visits and not knowing where your man is from one minute to the next.

In my younger days, it was a status thing to be able to namedrop which gang member you knew or were dating. It felt like protection to be associated with dangerous people (which, looking back, is ironic, seeing as it actually makes you far more vulnerable). They have nice cars and bundles of cash and you are too young and naive to realize that financially stable people don't carry thousands of pounds in their pockets and spend it all on designer clothes that sit in a wardrobe in the council bedsit they were given after leaving jail. It can all seem quite glamorous. But if he can buy you Loubs but can't get approved for credit, then his money is essentially worthless. You cannot create a future with it.

And you certainly can't create a future with someone whose workplace health-and-safety risks are murder or prison. Don't think about subjecting children to that lifestyle. The risks associated with being with a roadman fuckboy far outweigh the rewards. It can be very difficult to leave, much like all abusive relationships, but a specific factor with roadmen is that they may have access to weapons and it's harder to call the police because you may have been party to some of their crimes and are scared about implicating yourself. You may also be in a world where it is seen as snitching to call the police. You will need professional support, because your involvement in this relationship probably stems from childhood experiences around power dynamics and the normalization of abuse and control as well as crime. The police are very unlikely to charge you with anything if your purpose in approaching them is fear for your safety. But you do not *have to* call the police; talk to domestic abuse services about your options if you are in a situation you can't get out of.

People can reform from a life of crime, so ex-criminals who can show that they have graduated completely from the road life are worth giving a chance – unless their criminal history involved domestic or sexual violence. But there is nothing sexy about a man who is currently hiding cocaine in his bum hole, so be aware of active roadmen.

No-labels fuckboy

The no-labels fuckboy is problematic only if you are looking for something more than casual. He's rather a swaggerous fellow, generally someone fairly attractive and charming who finds it easy to get dates. He's probably telling you he has recently come out of a long-term relationship or that he is massively busy with work, so he is 'not looking for anything heavy right now', but he is happy to date and take things slowly, to see what the future holds. You will be cool with this suggestion because, in the early stages, you won't have caught feelings yet, so it sounds doable. The idea of taking things slowly gives you hope. You may think that what he says at this stage doesn't matter because, eventually, you will entice him to be your boyfriend with your delightful personality and life-changing vagina. But let me make it very clear: if he explicitly tells you that he's not looking for more than sex and he offers no glimmer of hope for a relationship, if you end up getting involved and getting hurt, that's not because he's a fuckboy, it's because you didn't listen.

The no-labels fuckboy is confusing because he makes you feel like you have really sparked his interest. Despite being clear that he is not looking for a relationship 'right now' (he always offers that glimmer of hope), he treats you as the first woman who has come along in a while to grab his attention. He's responsive, interested and invested in talking to you every day. Initial conversations go on for hours. You speak so often that it doesn't seem weird or creepy when he brings a bit of sex talk into the mix. He makes it clear that he's a sexual guy and would love to find someone who could match his appetite. You find yourself emphasizing how open about sex you are, because he is vocal about needing a woman who isn't childish and who owns her sexuality. He drops tiny hints about insane sexual chemistry – how it's hard not to fall in love when you find that with a woman. He showers you with compliments.

> **You leave these conversations feeling like a spectacular buff ting.**

The first date goes well. He may have suggested that it happen at either of your homes, but not always, because that can make his intentions too obvious. Often, no-labels fuckboy takes you out for dinner or drinks, which, coupled with the frequent communication, gives you the impression that he is interested in more than sex. By the end of the first date – or maybe the second, if you are determined not to sleep with him or were on your period during the first – you will feel like there is nothing more natural in the world than shagging this guy. The length of time you've been talking, plus the clear spark, means that sex will only solidify what the two of you have. He talked all night about how sexy you were and about places he wants to take you to in the future so you feel all fanny-fluttery and totally willing to jump into bed with him. This isn't the kind of dickish guy to fuck and run.

The next day you get a text saying he had a great time and you feel relieved that he is still interested. However, over the next few days you feel a palpable shift. He is not the same as he was. He's still checking in on you every now and then and responding to messages, but his replies take longer and his life appears to have become far busier. He gives you just enough attention to make you question whether you are over-analysing the change. He still chucks a few compliments your way, usually sexual ones, so you're certain he still likes you, even though the dynamic has shifted.

Infatuation creeps in (possibly limerence; see Chapter 6). You find yourself watching his 'last seen' status, his activity on WhatsApp or checking his Instagram every eight minutes while freaking out about why he has changed. You'll find yourself battling with yourself over whether or not to message him.

My advice: don't. If you have to question whether you should text him, the answer is no.

It's possible that he gets in touch and suggests a date at the weekend, and you are thrilled. But on the day of the date, some ridiculous drama happens (flat tyre, family member taken ill, friend's mother dies) and he suddenly can't make it. Because you've had a wax and done your hair and make-up, you suggest he comes over after the drama is resolved so that the beautification has not been a waste of time. He arrives at midnight and leaves at 3 a.m., saying he can't stay because of work. This becomes the pattern of your situationship. In some NLFB situations, you may have sex regularly and spend lots of nights together, so you attach meaning to the fact that he stays the night. Or sometimes he doesn't even stick around in between – he goes silent after sex and only pops up when he wants more, and you place meaning on the fact that he keeps coming back. He keeps you in a state of stable ambiguity, a term coined by Esther

Perel that describes this type of situation perfectly. The contact is regular and consistent, but their feelings, and what you are, is ambiguous.

He may even take you out, introduce you to his friends (but not as his girlfriend) and stay in regular contact, but he will not put any official title on the relationship. You are 'hanging out' or 'seeing' each other. Every time he speaks to a friend while you are with him you have your ears pricked, waiting for him to say, 'I'm just with my girl.' But he doesn't. You'll be left trying to stop yourself from blurting out '*What are we?*' because you are afraid that doing so would fuck things up completely.

The no-labels fuckboy is probably sleeping with other women but will claim that he's allowed because he's not in a relationship. This can bring out the 'pick me' in us and we begin to view other women as competition. He says he likes you and likes what you've got but that he doesn't feel ready to commit or be tied down. The boyfriend label brings obligations and responsibilities, and he just does not want to feel like that. He wants fun and easy. How you feel is irrelevant, because he has decided that this is how it's going to be. Put pressure on him to give you a label or cause stress because you don't have one and he just ends it. You want to eventually get a relationship, so you keep your mouth shut. We often find ourselves playing 'wifey' to a no-label fuckboy. We showcase our premium 'wifey' skills to make him realize how great we would be as a girlfriend. We often give him the benefit of having a relationship *and* full licence to sleep with other people. Why would anyone want to change that? Having relationships with single men doesn't make them love you. Set your boundaries and take the ball out of their court.

Privileged fuckboy

Educated at Eton and Oxbridge or the like, this fuckboy is recognizable by his Barbour jacket, brogues and Queen's English accent. He comes from old money and has been raised with the belief that everyone can be wealthy if they work hard enough and that those who are poor are poor because they are lazy. Despite having all of life's opportunities handed to him on a plate, he believes that he is successful because of his own hard work. He calls his mother 'Mummy'. He is a Tory and proud of it. He scoffs at lefties and socialists and feels angry at the thought that anyone might expect those in higher tax brackets to fund free school meals. He will enjoy ruggers (rugby) and getting blotto with his pals at the races.

His entitlement and arrogance will show through on his dating app profile. He will list his education history very clearly. His bio will say something like 'If you use words like "bants" and think that liking Corbyn makes you hip, please swipe left.' He will think nothing of telling you that you have a jolly good rack on first meeting. He will click his fingers at waiters and laugh at their mispronunciation of 'foie gras'. He believes in traditional gender roles and will expect the woman he marries to be happy to raise the children while doing a little philanthropy on the side. He will say things like 'Be a good girl and get me a drink, will you?' before tapping you on the bottom. He is elitist and has a superiority complex. He thinks he is better than everyone by virtue of his bloodline and inherited wealth. He treats working-class women extremely poorly and will make jokes about chavs being easy to sleep with, if you don't mind the smell. He enjoys sexist and racist banter and Priti Patel is his celeb crush. He knows that he can get away with anything because nothing that he has ever been accused of before has stuck. He is well connected and has enough money to hire the best lawyers, so groping random women comes without consequence. He has attachment issues stemming from his boarding-school experiences and he can often be cold and controlling. He has narcissistic tendencies and will look down on you if you got a 2:1 degree from an inner-city university. He will never care about a partner as much as he cares about himself; his lack of empathy is not just directed towards working-class people, he finds it hard to empathize with anyone. He will have a stiff-upper-lip attitude towards everything, so don't expect anything from him when you are doubled up with period pains.

> This type of fuckboy uses his privilege to undermine and belittle those who he believes are less than him – and pretty much every woman apart from his mummy is less than him in his eyes.

He uses it to get away with misogyny and sexually aggressive behaviour, and his connections to power and influential people mean that, most of the time, it works. He feels entitled to women in the same way that he feels entitled to pretty much everything.

Wasteman fuckboy

The wasteman fuckboy is defined by the fact that he relies entirely on the women he dates to support him financially. It's okay to be unemployed and to date unemployed people – life comes at you hard and fast and unemployment can hit anyone at any time; there should be no judgement of this. However, there are scenarios in which perpetual unemployment isn't just an unfortunate life turn, it's a lifestyle choice, and if we are dating those people, then we really do have to ask ourselves why we're okay with financially supporting Gary while he works on his mix tapes and contributes absolutely nothing apart from regular penis.

This guy will move into your house after the third date without you even realizing. You will think it's because you've fallen in love and can't get enough of each other but, really, it's because he's experiencing homelessness, though he won't tell you that. There will be some story about how he had a house but that it all fell through somehow (through no fault of his own) and so he has unexpectedly ended up having to stay at his nan's/brother's/cousin's place, but it's cool because he's got this amazing flat lined up and will be moving in soon. Then ensues a complicated story about how someone he knows is moving out of somewhere else so he has to wait until they leave before he can move in. So you think that it's all fine, because it's only temporary. You'll go off to work all day and he will be at home smoking weed and playing FIFA. If he manages to hoover while you're gone, it'll fool you into thinking that he's really improving your life and you might end up overlooking the fact that you are fostering a grown man. He will make you believe that he is destined for greatness; he's thirty-five and hasn't got anywhere yet, but he's certain that his latest Soundcloud upload is going to change everything. He works hard on his pipedreams, leaving him no time to earn any money except for the cash he makes from doing odd jobs for his mate once every three months. He is the type who can't hold down full-time work due to his attitude – he hates being told what to do. He hates feeling like anyone is his boss and so he argues or refuses to follow instructions. He doesn't want to work for the man so, despite having no prior knowledge or experience, he believes that he is going to build an empire and become CEO of his own business, without having to do any hard graft to get there.

If he has children with another woman, he will definitely continue to sleep with her. He can't contribute anything other than dick to her household, but she tolerates him for the sake of the kids. He needs her so that he has a regular place to sleep and eat if all else fails. He will not let that relationship of convenience end, even when he gets a girlfriend. Or several girlfriends, because a wasteman needs to maximize the number of women who are buying clothes and topping up his pay-as-you-go phone. And if he hasn't got any other female options, he will be intent on moving in with you and becoming reliant on you very quickly.

The wasteman fuckboy will never tell you that he's broke or ask for money; he will slyly convince you to offer it instead. There will always be some reason for his lack of funds on any particular day – something will have gone drastically wrong, like he's lost his bank card or he's had to pay his kid's mum £400 this month to cover school uniforms (lies) and that has left him a bit short. He'll drop hints about feeling terrible that he can't take you out and about how he might not be able to stay at yours for

MOTHERHOOD IS HARD

BUT IT'S EVEN

HARDER WHEN YOUR

ADOPTED CHILD

IS A

GROWN MAN

a while because he won't have the money to travel, and so of course you, being the kind and nurturing person that you are, will offer to lend him some. You will top up his travel card and make up a Tupperware box for him to have for lunch the next day. You will pay for meals at restaurants (because if you don't, the two of you would never go anywhere), and this will eventually become a habit. He will talk a good talk about his big plans for the future, though, so you will feel that you are helping him through a rough patch and that he will be on his feet soon.

The wasteman fuckboy is usually fantastic in bed – he needs to be, to ensure that women keep begging him to come back. It's his currency. Dick really is the only thing that he has to offer.

> A wasteman can seem great at the start, because he's always around, but don't get fooled, he's not always around because he's falling for you and can't be away from you, it's because he's got fuck all else to do and he wants your food.

It is important to think about what kind of life you can build with someone who relies on you to feed them. Motherhood is hard, but it's even harder when your adopted child is a grown man. If you come across one of these fuckboys, you need to be googling the number for your local waste removal service asap.

Abusive fuckboy

Danger! Fucking danger!

Heed the early warning signs with these fuckboys and take action as soon as you spot them. Please do not think that violence is only physical; often it's not. Control is violence; emotional abuse is violence; sexual control or abuse is violence; financial control is violence; the threat of violence is violence. If you experience any of these things, you are in a violent relationship even if he's never hit you. There is no prototype for abusive fuckboys, no dress code or other physically identifiable features. The violent/controlling fuckboy can come in any shape or size, age, ethnicity or class, from any walk of life (as can all of these fuckboys, except for perhaps the privileged fuckboy, who can only come from one walk of life).

He usually starts out behaving like the perfect man, lulling you into a false sense of security. You fall for him quickly; you think you have found your dream guy, a man who compliments you, wants to be with you, calls you loads, FaceTimes you when he's not with you and wants to pick you up after nights out to keep you safe. The speed and intensity of the relationship is much faster than with any other fuckboy category. He makes you feel wanted and needed. Within the first few days or weeks, you sense you've met your soulmate. You've never felt safer with anyone and it seems nothing can go wrong. He has reeled you into a fantasy relationship, playing a character that bears little relation to his true self. This is called 'love bombing'.

Once you are head over heels for him, you begin to notice that he's unnecessarily jealous of or focused on asking about your exes or other men. He may start accusing you of flirting with men on nights out or asking you who you are texting every time you use your phone. He might get angry over you spilling a drink, holding it against you for days. The abusive fuckboy likes to use the silent treatment – sometimes for days or weeks – over minor misdemeanours, which forces you to feel you have to apologize even when you've done nothing wrong. He starts arguments when you want to go out or accuses you of dressing like a slut when you do. He may pull you up about having too much cleavage on show in an Instagram pic. He says nasty things about your friends, accusing them of being 'loose' or 'easy', and warns you what people must think of you for hanging out with them. He can convince you to stop socializing with them because he believes that people will judge you a hoe by association or he will convince you that they are really your enemies.

You barely go out any more because it's just not worth the shit he gives you when you do.

The abusive fuckboy likes to put you down, to belittle you both at home and in public. He chips away at your confidence with negging remarks or blatant criticisms. He makes you seem inferior in front of friends and family. He may also become irrationally jealous of your relationship with them. A friend of mine had a violent boyfriend who accused her of having sex with her dad because she slept over at her father's house one night. The abusive fuckboy accuses you of being interested in male colleagues and kicks off if your male manager messages you outside of work. He may be nasty to your pet and threaten to harm it if you don't submit to his demands. He may also use the pet to make you stay.

The violent or controlling abusive fuckboy may use drugs or drink heavily and blames those substances for his outbursts. He also blames you for his bad moods. Everything he does is your fault. He may punch walls, throw things or drive recklessly while you are in the car to scare you. He is destroying your confidence and putting you in a position where you constantly feel you must prove your love for him.

The abusive fuckboy has probably opened up to you about his troubled childhood or previous trauma. You have empathy for him. He balances out the violent or controlling incidents with occasional spells of really lovely behaviour. He seeks to blame the bad behaviour on those sad times in his previous life. He manipulates you into sympathizing with him. You come under fire for his outbursts because you provoked or triggered him. He will express remorse after particularly bad episodes, and this will convince you that there is hope for change.

He has reeled you into a fantasy relationship, playing a character that bears little relation to his true self.

His behaviour will have dramatically shifted from how it was at the beginning. But because you are now emotionally invested, and because he makes you feel like the change in his behaviour is your fault, you stick around, believing that things will go back to how they were at the start. Sometimes they do; sometimes he makes you feel amazing, sometimes he is kind, sometimes you have moments when you remember why you fell for him, and those moments are just enough to keep you hanging on. But it's not the only thing that keeps you there. You think you can't leave because you know that he won't let you, or because you are financially dependent on him, or because he has ground your self-esteem down so low that you believe that nobody else could ever want you or that you could never have a successful relationship because the way you are being treated is what you deserve.

The abusive fuckboy will often have sex with you whether you want to or not. This is rape, even if you are in a relationship. He works on making you feel like your body is disgusting and unworthy. He might also be physically violent towards you – anything from hard pinches and grips to full-on beating.

This man could take your life someday. He really could.

Two women are killed in England and Wales every week of the year by violent partners or ex-partners. Even if he doesn't kill you, in treating you like this, he's already robbing you of your life.

It is very hard to leave the abusive fuckboy because he threatens your safety when you do – or threatens to kill himself. (This is very common, but it is never your responsibility to save him from himself.) He's quite capable of stalking and harassing you if you end the relationship. He's ready to try to ruin your future relationships or – better yet – make you believe that nobody else will ever want you. But you *can* leave. It *can* be done. People can and do survive domestic violence and come out the other side stronger. The respect I have for those people is immense, because it takes a lot to flee. That's why I advise running at the first sign, before you get caught in his trap. I cannot overemphasize how key it is to recognize love bombing – too much too soon is a red flag and when it turns suddenly from an intense whirlwind you must run, not try to reverse the change.

These fuckboys are by far the worst of all. Under no circumstances give him further chances to change once you have spotted any of the warning signs. You must protect yourself and your children, if you have them, and safely leave. Leaving is the most dangerous time, so it is important to develop a safety plan with professionals if possible. If you are dealing with this, please try to seek help. My podcast with Women's Aid may help with this (follow the link to the podcast in my Instagram bio). There are also confidential support services available in your local area – google them or talk to a friend or relative if you can't seek professional support. You have nothing to feel ashamed or embarrassed about and you are not to blame for any of it.

If reading all of this has left you feeling deflated and depressed about the fact that the world is full of these men, then I want you to remember that this knowledge of them gives you power. You have now identified a full list of red flags for most of the potential fuckboys that you will encounter, and this is part of your anti-fuckboy toolkit. Instead of feeling worried that these people exist, we need to feel empowered by the fact that we are able to identify them and are therefore in a much stronger position to be able to avoid them.

This knowledge gives you power.

Chapter 5:

Wherefore art thou, Romeo?

Where are all the decent men? All the good men I know are married or gay. I have tried all the apps and I hate them equally, but I really would like a partner, so I am not ready to give up. Are some apps better than others? Is there some kind of secret to matching good blokes? Could my bio be the problem?

*I*f you know that you are ready to meet someone, whether it be for love, sex or simply because your phone has been a bit dry and you feel like having a flirt, then you have to figure out where to find them. Dating apps have changed everything. We all used to meet organically, at uni, in bars, through friends – there was no other choice – but it is now estimated that by 2035 more than half of all relationships will have started online.[6] If you have been using the apps, then you are probably aware that the dating pool is pretty grim, especially if you are over thirty – it's less of a pool and more like a toilet. We have already discussed misogyny and the multitude of fuckboy types that are clogging up the pool. So why the fuck would anyone want to jump into this toilet? Well, if you know that a partner is something you feel would enhance your life and you are certain that swimming alongside the turds are kind, loving, loyal, honest, intelligent, lovely men, then it's worth dipping your toe into the sewer. Good men do exist: we just have to figure out where they are and we also have to be open to meeting them.

IRL

One of the reasons it's becoming less common to meet in real life is because, when you do go out, everybody is glued to their phone. They barely even talk to their own dinner companions, prioritizing taking photos of their food, so talking to strangers is even more rare. I also feel that, as you get older, people are less likely to approach you randomly.

---

6   'Finding love online: More than half of couples set to meet via the internet'. Sky News, 27 November 2019. https://news.sky.com/story/finding-love-online-more-than-half-of-couples-set-to-meet-via-the-internet-11871341

THE DATING
POOL IS LESS
OF A POOL
AND MORE

LIKE A
TOILET

Not because you are less attractive, but because you are more likely to tell them to fuck off. Being approached does still happen, though, and I would highly recommend being a bit bolder when it does. What I mean is, if you walk past someone or sit opposite them on a train and you really fancy them and keep exchanging flirtatious glances or smiles, then it can feel like an absolute tragedy to lose them simply because you were too shy to say something. This has happened to me many times; I've walked past a guy and we have both kept looking back over our shoulders but, because I felt self-conscious, I've just continued marching on. Then I spend the next two days kicking myself for potentially losing the love of my life due to my awkwardness. More recently, I have tried a different approach when these situations happen: I have turned, stopped and given the nod and we have ended up exchanging numbers. All while I was bright red and shaky, which didn't seem to put them off. This kind of thing can happen anywhere – from the street to the supermarket. I always put on a bit of mascara when I go to Tesco, just in case my soulmate happens to be in aisle six. You could also fill your basket with a bottle of wine, a ready meal for one, a cucumber and some Vaseline if you want to make sure that all the eligible shoppers definitely know you're single.

Bars, pubs, gigs, festivals and the like are all obvious places to meet potential partners. You could tactically try to time your visit to the pub with a football or boxing match screening to maximize the number of men who will be there, however you will probably be largely ignored until it's over. Bars tend to be better than pubs, but then there is the whole awkwardness of having to shout over music to be heard. Gigs are great because you know you have at least one thing in common but, again, it's loud and people are usually with friends so it's not always easy to get talking. Outdoor festivals are good for meeting like-minded people, but that only gives you a three-month window every year.

Work is another opportunity to attract a partner, although I don't recommend this one; it's like shitting on your own doorstep. It's really fun at first (work romance, that is, not shitting on your doorstep); having a work crush makes going into work feel like an exciting adventure, though getting ready every morning becomes a monumental task. Hiding it from colleagues brings a bit of a sexy and dangerous element while also bonding you and your partner with a shared secret. It's all fun and games, until it's not. A bad break-up with someone you still have to see *every single day* is traumatic, to say the least, and it can lead to all sorts of career-based stress. If you're working a summer job that you don't care about, then it's not such an issue, but if you are in a career that you have worked hard for and that you take seriously, it's worth giving it some thought before jumping into office romances.

Having a hobby is an excellent way to meet like-minded people. Whether it's pottery, running, cooking, singing – whatever floats your boat – look for a local club and sign up. Get involved. Meet new people. Even if there are no potential partners there, there are still potential friends and, you never know, they might have a hot eligible sibling or friend. The gym is a pretty good hotspot too, plus it means that if they fancy you while you're a sweaty mess, then you're definitely good to go when you meet and you look normal. Volunteering is even better; you can give something back to the community while potentially meeting a love interest. The Royal Voluntary Service has lots of opportunities.

Love is not just something that we gain from having romantic partners, though; we can obtain it from a variety of sources, so helping out with a cause in your community is a sure-fire way to tap into a huge source of soul connection that can help to alleviate the emptiness we sometimes feel when we lack romantic love. bell hooks writes wisely about this in *All About Love*: community, spirituality, family, friends, work – reciprocal love can be found in loads of places. When you are loving, you are generating love, so just getting out there and throwing yourself into things you enjoy makes being single feel fantastic and opens you up to more opportunities for love. If you can fill yourself up from other sources before heading out into the wild, I can guarantee you will be in a better headspace when you face some of the more depressing sides of dating. Finding other forms of love, including self-love, is an incredible fuckperson filter.

Another potential meeting place for romance outside of the designated dating apps is on social media: Instagram, Twitter, Facebook and the rest. Sliding into DMs is common now and, while Instagram isn't specifically a dating app, it's certainly a platform on which you can meet potential partners. But slide cautiously – because, unlike dating apps, people aren't there looking for love/sex. Perhaps if you see someone say something in a comments section that you really agree with, or you see someone tagged in a picture with a friend and you think they are attractive, check out their page and establish if they're single. Give out a few tactical likes and away you go.

Regardless of how you meet, whether it's in person or online, the way someone talks to you is very important. I feel that it's stating the obvious to say that if their opening line involves complimenting your bum, boobs or body, or if it's overtly sexual, then this person is not likely to be looking for a long-term relationship. I used to be flattered by that kind of thing. I hated being sexually objectified by men who I wasn't interested in, but if I fancied the man giving me sexualized 'compliments', I thought it was okay, a great sign that he thought I was potential 'wifey material'. It didn't occur to me that the very fact that he thought it was perfectly reasonable to approach a stranger in a sexual manner was a red flag. I didn't see it as such because I was still catering to the male gaze, aspiring to be sexy and therefore, I thought, valuable. I had no idea.

As a general point, when you're out in the world, basic respect is immensely important. Catcalling from cars or down the street is disrespectful, as is grabbing your arm or entering your personal space in a dominant way. Any approach that suggests a man doesn't recognize that women are often subjected to unwanted catcalls and street harassment is worrying. Sometimes, saying no to a man who is asking for your number can be terrifying – some will say that you're ugly anyway, some may refuse to take no for an answer, some may not give up unless you tell them you have a boyfriend (because they are more likely to respect an imaginary man than a real-life woman). It can feel paralysing. Men should be conscious of this and act accordingly, with respectful approaches.

> **Of course, we all want to be fancied and desired by the people we are attracted to, but we should expect them to be able to contain their excitement until a clear green light has been given.**

To approach in an aggressive, dominant or sexual way, whether online or in real life, gives a good indication of how a man views women, which is in turn a good indication of how he will ultimately treat you.

Dating apps

Dating apps are the most obvious route to go down if you are actively looking for love, sex or anything else in between. They are convenient, for one thing; you don't have to leave your house and you can suss people out a bit before meeting in person. But while lots of successful relationships have started online, I'm not sure I know anyone who would say they enjoy the experience of using dating apps – most people find them either stressful or dull. A lot of people follow the familiar pattern of downloading and deleting the apps on a regular cycle. After a while, you jump off and vow never to do it again . . . until six months later, when you're bored or feel like you need a bit of attention.

Dating apps can feel really soul-destroying, but they don't have to. I think that the biggest thing to remember is that everyone is having similar experiences: you're not the only one who is getting matches but no messages, or barely any matches at all, or people who match and then unmatch, or weird sexual opening messages. It's not you; it's not that you're not good enough. It's not happening because you're ugly or unworthy. It's literally happening left, right and centre, to the vast majority of women on there, and we need to not internalize it.

> **It's Tinder that's shit, not you.**

But amazing people *can* be found on the apps, so it's worth using them if you know that you're really ready for somebody amazing. We just have to know how to filter out the crap ones.

Some apps are definitely better than others. People often suggest that you might find more serious men on the paid apps like Match.com, but I have heard from a ridiculous number of women who have met married men on paid apps (don't get me wrong, married men are on free apps too; it's just preferable not to pay to meet them). Tinder is hard work because apparently there is a huge misconception that it's a hook-up site, so you have to constantly explain that you are looking to date, not casually shag (unless you're looking to casually shag, obviously). My male friends tell me that Tinder is a place to go to meet women for sex. I think a lot of women have downloaded Tinder under the impression that we will find potential life partners on there, and while I know a few people who have successfully done just that, there are a lot of conversations that go something like this:

> **Him:** *So what are you looking for on here? [FYI, I believe this question is often an indication that they don't want anything serious]*
>
> **Us:** *I'm looking to date, hopefully meet someone that I click with. I'm not looking for casual at the moment. How about you?*
>
> **Him:** *Ah that's cool. So how big are your tits, babe?*

It's exhausting. Plenty of Fish is even worse, though. Ninety per cent of the men on POF look like they screenshot their profile picture from Myspace. Men on POF mainly display selfies, but terrible ones – usually taken on a webcam in a dimly lit room with wallpaper peeling off in the background and while wearing an ill-fitting suit jacket and an Adidas cap, holding up two fingers in a sort of attempted gun finger pose. Bumble and Hinge tend to be the sites that cis-het women prefer: the profile pictures tend to be more modern and up to date, and women have to make the first move on Bumble, so they aren't bombarded with messages in the same way, while Hinge gives you a bit more to work with because to sign up you have to fill out lots of stuff in your bio – but they aren't much different to Tinder in that there's often an underlying sense that casual sex is the preferred option for most of the male users.

Pictures on dating apps are key, and I think they are to blame for why so many people struggle to find decent matches. It puts me off if a guy only has selfies, especially if they were all taken on the same day, just him and three different angles of his face, and that's made worse if he's pouting or biting/licking his lips in an attempt to look sexy or if he looks like he just accidentally turned on the front-facing camera but posted the picture anyway. And it's even worse if those selfies are taken in front of a dirty mirror with the flash on or in front of an unmade bed in a messy room. It just shows me that they have no self-awareness or motivation to present themselves at their best.

I like to see pictures that show evidence that the man has friends and a life outside of his bedroom – as long as the snaps with friends don't show them with a Gucci man bag across their bare chest, all pointing at each other while holding bottles of Grey Goose. Or stroking a sedated tiger. Or holding up a traumatized-looking fish and high-fiving. I don't know why men feel the need to point at each other in so many pictures, or why they want to be captured with drinks and animals – only certain animals, though, never gerbils or hamsters.

It's interesting, because I've met men in real life who I've fancied but then I've seen their social media and thought, 'If I'd have seen these pics on an app, it would have been a hard no.' Trying to meet people based on the 2D image we are presented with can end up making us reject people who really might be a good match. I hate apps and wish that we could go back to a time when meeting in real life was the only option so we didn't have to choose between Gary's close-up selfie of his nostrils and Gareth's topless picture at Ocean Beach, but here we are.

You also need to think about your own profile. What do you want to put out there? We will be judged on our pictures, and the ones we choose make a statement. Smiling is super-important; it makes you look happy and approachable. Think about the profile pictures you have seen where the person looks utterly miserable in every picture – it doesn't really draw you in. Think about choosing five pictures that show you doing things that make you happy. In terms of clothes, you could be dressed in a full-body smock and men would still act like predators, but it is realistic to say that the more skin you have on show, the more assumptions will be made about your intentions on the app. Which is patriarchal bullshit, obviously, but it's still a sad fact of life. Somehow, many cis-het men have not yet managed to catch up to the fact that clothes in no way indicate anything about your sex life. So, wear what you like, but be ready to shut down the inevitable abundance of slimy roaches that come with sexier pictures.

Dating profile bios are equally as important, and we must think about this when creating our own. I think the best ones are those that give an idea of what you're into: your interests, hobbies, the kind of music you like, if you're particularly religious or a vegan who wouldn't date a carnivore. But before you even get to this stage you should be quite clear about what it is that you are looking for. What do you *really* want? Are you open to meeting anyone and seeing what happens, whether it's something casual or something more? Or are you quite clear that you want to date with a view to a partnership? Do you have a list of non-negotiables? These are important, and they shouldn't be about looks and physical attraction. To me, it is very important that I am on the same page intellectually and politically as any potential date. It will be different for everyone, but some things you might consider are: Are they a feminist? Are they actively anti-racist? Does climate change matter to them? Are they religious? Are you hugely into travelling and know that you need someone who is willing and able to jet off at the drop of a hat? Whatever it is, if these things deeply matter to you, then it should be non-negotiable that they matter to a partner and that you share a world view.

However, listing the things that you want or don't want should be done in a way that doesn't sound too prescriptive or negative; and it shouldn't suggest that anyone who doesn't meet your criteria is gross. Have you ever seen profiles where men make lists of what they want in a woman? Have a scroll on any dating app and it won't take long before you come across a man who looks like he's had the same haircut since 1973 stating that he wants a woman who is feminine (not feminist), natural, no make-up but makes an effort, slim but curvy, doesn't take herself too seriously but places her career over her looks, takes pride in her appearance but doesn't plaster her photos over social media, is a good listener but isn't too loud . . . the lists are endless and are designed to make women who don't meet their ridiculous list of demands feel inferior. But they are a useful way to filter out the wankers. Just make sure that your non-negotiables are set out in a non-wankerish way. So instead of saying, 'Looking for a man who doesn't murder animals for his dinner,' you could say, 'I'm vegan and would prefer a partner with a plant-based diet.'

Our fundamental morals and values are important. It is not a case of having to agree on everything: healthy debate and differing opinions are great, but not when it comes to the really big stuff – like definitely knowing that you never want to have children – and particularly if that stuff has a direct impact on other human beings.

> Homophobia, transphobia, racism, ableism, classism, fatphobia, antisemitism, Islamophobia – basically any -ism that makes someone believe that they are superior to any other human – is a major red flag for relationships.

If you don't fit into any of the groups of people they dislike and therefore think that you can tolerate their vile beliefs because they don't affect you, you need to reflect more on what all that really means. It's very much tied up in the patriarchy and is a huge indicator for narcissism. It shows a lot about their character and how they will function in a relationship. Nothing good can come from a relationship with someone who supports political systems that oppress people or who carries irrational hate or a lack of empathy for others. Establish their views on this stuff early on – it's at the core of who they are.

Listen to what men say on their profiles. If you know that you aren't looking for hook-ups, do not match with people who say they aren't looking for anything serious in their bio, even if they are insanely attractive. Hang on to what they are clearly stating about the present – the future might involve them getting run over by a bus; who knows? It's just not worth clinging on to a maybe. Guys who are upfront about their intentions for casual hook-ups on the apps are not fuckboys. Apps are perfect for meeting people for fun; it's only an issue when they lie about their intentions in order to get someone into bed.

Some red flags for the covert sex desperados are:

- **Every compliment they give you is about your appearance**
- **They're not interested in getting to know you and so ask only banal questions**
- **They ask for lots of pictures and hint at wanting to see 'naughtier ones'**
- **They want dates to be home-based rather than in public**
- **They constantly try to steer the conversation in a sexual direction.**

There are a few brilliant accounts on Instagram that analyse dating app profiles and messages in depth. I would recommend @tindertranslators, @thirtysomethingsingle and @singleblackwoman_x for more on this.

I think it's important to go on to dating apps with a thick skin. Expect to be cussed, because it happens often. Men will jump in your inbox saying something like 'You look proper filthy, u got a face I'd like to cum on,' or 'That must have been an accidental match. You're punching well above your weight looool.' Instead of it feeling like a dent to your self-esteem, it should feel like, 'Ah, I was expecting to come across an incel or two on here, and here we are.' When I say 'expect to be cussed', I don't mean you need to tolerate it, I just mean that when it happens you need to know that this is not happening because of you. It's a commonly used technique called negging (a favourite of narcissists). 'Negging' is a term coined by pick-up artists – men who share tips online for the best ways to get a woman into bed. They use elements of neuro-linguistic programming and psychology to manipulate and seduce. They are a terrifying group of men. They recommend negging as one of their core tactics. The theory is that making us feel bad about ourselves, bringing us down a peg or two, knocks our confidence, so we are more likely to be vulnerable to their advances, especially when they follow up a negative comment with a compliment. It makes you feel insecure and worry that something about you is unattractive while at the same time making you feel grateful that, despite this, they still find you attractive. We begin to need their validation. An example of negging might be if you're talking to a guy and he mentions that you look really hot in a particular picture but then starts to joke about the size of your feet, or that you have a beautiful face and he bets you were gorgeous when you were younger.

Kelechi Okafor notes that Black women who match with non-Black men online often have to face a form of racial negging: 'You're pretty for a dark-skin girl,' or 'You think a man like me could handle all that big African booty?' Fetishization is equally common and equally negative: white men telling Black women that they are a 'chocolate queen', non-disabled men telling disabled women that they find their disability hot, men telling fat women that they are obsessed with 'BBW's, constantly bringing the conversation back to their 'huge ass'. When you shut this grim fetishizing down, they will act like you should be grateful for the compliment. It is always disguised as banter or flirtation, and if you complain, you will be accused of not being able to take a joke. It is important to watch out for this in the early stages, and it is especially important not to take it personally. This shit is rife. There is a high chance that you will be made to feel bad about yourself at some point.

It's tactical, it's nasty and it's no reflection on you. Don't allow it to get into your head. Report them on the apps, then **block, delete, move on**. Don't engage with the negging. They want you to be upset; they enjoy it. Do not internalize the nasty comments from dating-app trolls; they mean nothing.

Dating with a disability adds far greater challenges to the already rough ride. I discussed this with Joy Addo (@joysworldthepodcast) and Cathy Reay (@thatsinglemum) on my podcast (link in my IG bio). Both women have a disability and we talked at length about the way that ableism and disability impacts on dating. Cathy said: 'Quite often, your disability might limit you from being able to meet people in a club, or the kind of environment where we would normally meet people pre-apps or off-apps. I think, for me, it feels really good to be able to put myself out there and not know who's rejecting me. They see me, automatically, and then they swipe right if they like me, and they swipe left if they don't, and that's fine, I don't get to see who swipes left, so I can never be hurt by it. I just know that whoever I match with is okay with it, and it kind of takes away that initial discomfort of whether he can get over the fact that I'm disabled.'

Joy advised, 'It's really good to be confident in your disability. You have to own it. If you are worried about it and you find it a problem, why would the other person not find it a problem? They're going to take the vibe from you. So, if you're like, "You know what, this is my disability, this is how it affects me," it's like, "Okay, cool, let's move on." It's a part of you, but it's not who you are.' Follow both of these wonderful women for more on this topic.

Decent people on the apps will come with respectful conversation that suggests they are interested in you as a person and not just in what you can give them or what you look like. It is super-common for men on dating apps to ask questions which seek solely to establish whether you can fulfil their idea of the perfect mother–wife hybrid, for example: Can you cook? When are you going to cook for me? Can you give good massages? How would you impress me? It annoys the shit out of me; a man will not want to know anything at all about my career, my life or my interests, he just wants to know if I can carry out basic life tasks that benefit him.

> **I am not a carer for incapable men.**

I enjoy cooking for my partners and giving them massages. But they are both things that I want to do for my man when I am ready. You can want to cater to your partner and still be a feminist, if you are catering to them because you love it, not because they expect you to by virtue of your gender. If a man asks constant questions like this it shows that he's already assigned you a role without taking the time to get to know you as a person. He doesn't care whether you have anything in common, so long as you can cook a roast dinner and give him a blow job.

Once you do get speaking to someone who hasn't cussed or otherwise offended you, it is essential to ask if they have any other social media that you could contact them on before you consider exchanging numbers. We can establish a lot from a quick Google search; however, what you find will only be useful if they have given you their real details, which is why befriending them on social media is important. In this day and age, it is unusual not to have social media, so if they say they don't, it's potentially a red flag (of course, some people aren't on social media at all, but it's pretty rare to not at least be on LinkedIn). Check to ensure that the profiles they do have seem legit: do they have a range of friends and family, or do all their followers look like random people they've met on apps? It is very easy to lift pictures from someone else's Instagram, so check if they have tagged friends in pictures and if they are interacting with real people. In the early stages of talking, it is important to keep in the back of your mind that the person in the pictures might not be who you are talking to. They might be a catfish. A catfish is someone who pretends to be someone else online. You might think you're talking to 32-year-old Charlie, a finance executive from Balham, when it's really Carl, a 72-year-old scientist from Slough who has a penchant for roleplaying young men on dating apps. I find it quite easy to spot them now – they say they have no social media, but their pictures are filtered and framed and you can tell that those pictures are from Instagram. Catfishes usually use really hot pictures that make them look like models and they always state their profession as property developers, doctors or lawyers. But their bios often don't match up to that. I don't know any lawyers who would write, 'Looking 4 a queen, don't want no penpals.' Other signs of catfishing are not wanting to video call, not being available to meet face to face, setting up dates then ghosting or making constant excuses as to why they have had to cancel.

Catfishes can be very dangerous; many of them are scammers. In 2020, online romance fraud cost victims £63,000,000 in the UK, according to Action Fraud.[7] If you receive a random DM or Facebook request from a man who claims to be a Texan army general who is looking after his sick son all alone and needs to get him to the UK for treatment at Great Ormond Street Hospital and who falls in love with you very quickly and sends you his Western Union money transfer link, then he is definitely a fraudulent criminal. They are often more subtle, though: they will build up a conversation over a long time then tell you that their mother has just died and they are struggling to raise cash for the funeral and you will feel compelled to offer them the money. Make sure they are who they say they are. You can Google reverse search their pictures to see if they appear elsewhere under another name, or you could ask them to send a picture doing something random like touching their ear while holding four fingers

7   Vittozzi, Katerina. 'Online romance fraud has cost victims £63m in 2020'. Sky News online, 26 December 2020. https://news.sky.com/story/online-romance-fraud-has-cost-victims-63m-in-2020-12172618

up – something they wouldn't easily be able to find among the pictures of the person they are pretending to be.

> **Be cautious about giving out too much information about your finances.**

Do not send money to people you have never met. We should not be loaning or giving money to people we have just met, even if we have been talking to them online for a while, and if they ask it's a big red flag.

Having no social media may also indicate that the man has a girlfriend or a wife. Once, I was halfway through a date when the man told me I had the exact same hair colour as his girlfriend. As I reeled away in shock, I asked why he hadn't told me he had a girlfriend and he casually replied that I hadn't asked. You would think it would be safe to assume that anyone you meet on a dating app is single, but it's really not. Nowadays, I always ask from the outset about the man's relationship status, and on several occasions the answer has been that they are in one. Sometimes, the answer has also been an incredulous 'Of course I'm single, why would I be on a dating app if I wasn't?' but I have later found out through social media searches that their version of single actually means married.

The cheaters will come up with all sorts of excuses if they are caught red-handed. They will claim that they are living with their ex for the sake of the kids, or they give you a sob story. One guy told one of my followers that he couldn't leave his wife because she wasn't able to care for their children safely without him being present. She later found out that his wife was a teacher, who clearly can keep children safe without assistance. We have to be very careful not to get bamboozled by bullshit – sadly, there are a lot of attached people on the apps. Their lies can be very convincing, so it is important to look out for the additional clues. They will often ask who you live with very early on; they want to know if they can come to your house, as you definitely cannot go to theirs. They might pop up to reply to messages only every few days. They don't want to arrange a date in their local area. They are weird about when they can speak to you, and on evenings and weekends they go a bit quiet. They can't answer your phone calls spontaneously or have random video chats.

> **This should go without saying, but if there is any hint of a man being involved with another woman, that should be your cue to run.**

If this is the first person you've matched and got along with and really fancied in a *really* long time and they are emphatically telling you they're single, yet all the flags are pointing to them not being so, it can be incredibly tempting to ignore the signs. But this will inevitably lead to disaster and heartbreak for you and everybody else involved. It's so much easier to shut it down at this point than it is further down the line, when his wife is banging down your door.

If you do get to the stage where you're having a good back-and-forth exchange, it's all going well and you're thinking, 'Finally! A normal one who's got social media, doesn't seem to have a girlfriend and is holding a decent conversation has come along,' it's devastating when they suddenly go and ruin it by coming out with completely out-of-context sexual stuff. For example, in reply to you talking about how exhausting your day at work was, he will say, 'Bet you need a massage all over that juicy backside, babe. Send me a pic of you in your uniform looking filthy' with the embarrassed-monkey emoji.

Previous me used to get led into sexual conversations because literally every man on dating apps steered things that way and, even though I knew that I wasn't there for casual sex, I also knew that to appeal to men I needed to prove that I was going to meet their desire for a woman who is a 'lady on the streets but a freak in the sheets'. I didn't want to come across as prudish because I'm not, so even though I was uncomfortable having conversations about sex that early, I felt

I would be giving the wrong impression if I completely shut it down. It took me a while to realize that if they are setting the tone that early on, then they're clearly showing their intentions and are not looking for a long-term relationship. If they really gave a shit about getting to know you, they'd be asking about your dreams and ambitions, not how big your nipples are.

When it's too much too soon, it's a massive turn-off. You will know your own limits, but I personally don't enjoy having any kind of sexual conversations until after I have met them in person. I have been on enough disappointing first dates to know that you just don't know if you will feel quite as sexual when you are face to face. I have learned to set my boundaries on this, but they all seem to respond in exactly the same way when you shut down premature sexting – it's as if they have a script. They'll say, 'Why are you being so serious?', or 'We're both adults', or they'll tell you to lighten up or ask if you're on your period. No, Gary, I just don't want to talk about my vagina to a stranger who appears to think that my fanny is the most interesting thing about me. Let me get to that stage; don't try to lead me there in order to judge how sexually liberated I am or how easy it will be to sleep with me, and do not fucking gaslight me by telling me to 'Calm down, it was only banter.' Would it be banter if I asked your mum how big her nipples were at the dinner table? No, so bring the same energy to your 'banter' with me.

It's the same with asking for nude pictures. Don't ask me for nudes or 'a cheeky pic', let me send them to you if and when I think you deserve them. However, I would advise strongly against sending nudes to people you barely know. It's potentially risky even in established relationships, but sending nudes to virtual strangers increases the risks massively. It can feel tempting, especially if a fanny-fluttering conversation has preceded, but you have to ask yourself, would I be okay with my dad seeing this on a porn site? Am I okay with this being shown to other strangers? How would I feel if everyone who follows me on IG saw this? The sad reality is that nudes get shared in group WhatsApps, on awful incel forums, all over the dark web, and they can be used against us. And while there is

If they really gave a shit about getting to know you, they'd be asking about your dreams and ambitions, not how big your nipples are.

no shame at all in sending pictures of your naked body and all the shame should be upon the person who leaked the nudes – which is a crime and should be reported – there are still personal ramifications to consider. If you really want to send one, then make sure it doesn't include your face or any identifying features like tattoos.

Another way that men often ruin things is with unsolicited dick pics.

It is such a shame when they spoil it all with a surprise willy.

It's happened to me on a couple of occasions. The conversation has been going well, I've been innocently talking about my love of books and they'll say something like 'I've got something you might like more than books ...' and *bam!*, all of a sudden, there's a little penis in my face and it's like, nope, a Roald Dahl book would excite me far more than that willy wonky any day. Then you have to block them because they've announced themselves as an unsexy flasher. There's something tragic about the image of them standing in their bedroom with their boxers round their ankles, willy in one hand, phone in the other, struggling to find the angle that shows the most girth and thinking, 'She's going to *love* this.' I've seen several guys photographing their dick next to a Sky remote to show off its length. I was more turned on by the remote . . . I can't wait for the day when they get the memo that it's really creepy and, as much as I can joke about it, it is actually a sex offence and a horrible violation. Most of us don't want to see a penis that we haven't consented to seeing. Out-of-context dicks are gross. BLOCK.

Shut it down

Here is where **block, delete, move on** comes into play. It seems obvious that if someone makes you feel bad about yourself, or they fetishize you, or they cross your sexual boundaries too soon, you would

simply end the conversation and
never look back. But it's easier
said than done. Especially if
you have it in your head that
you are the problem or if you
are dating because you desperately
don't want to be single, or sometimes

You have the power to cut out anyone who is making you feel less than amazing.

simply because you find them so fucking attractive you really don't
want to waste the match. It can be very easy to fall into the trap of
scolding them for their faux pas and trying to get past it. For example,
they give you a backhanded sexual compliment and instead of telling
them to fuck off, you tell them you didn't like it; they say it was just
banter so you feel silly for making an issue about it and you just carry
on. Or you have a strong suspicion that they have a girlfriend because
they have no social media and they are being funny about exchanging
numbers and, instead of following your gut, you listen to their wild
excuses and keep going.

At this stage, when you have only just started talking and there are no
feelings involved, it is so much easier to cut it off than it will be further
down the line. Any hint of red flags or any gut instinct that tells you that
something is off should be listened to. Take your power back and block –
on the app, on your phone and on social media. Blocking doesn't have to
come from a place of anger. It is simply done to ensure that they have no
means to get to you to try to persuade you that you made a mistake. Then
delete. Deleting their messages means that you have no trace of them on
your phone, so you won't be tempted to look back over the conversation
and be reminded of the horrible thing they said to you, and it means that
you can move on, taking with you the lessons you've learned and the
knowledge that you have the power to cut out anyone who is making you
feel less than amazing.

These hurdles are a sad reality of dating apps. But we can't change Tinder,
Hinge, Bumble and the rest; the only thing we can change is our mindset.

We must go into this with **spectacular buff ting** energy while retaining the knowledge that all the hurdles we face are not because we are lacking in any way but because dating is hard for everyone. Have regular breaks from the apps when they start to become a chore. Don't take any of the bullshit personally, and don't ever see it as a competition. Remind yourself that you are a **spectacular buff ting** and you've got this.

Chapter 6:

Twenty-first-century romance

I am newly dating after divorce and it feels like an assault course. I have been on Tinder for six months and, in that time, I have been ghosted twice after sex, catfished once and been contacted by a woman because I was unknowingly talking to her husband. I am no closer to finding love; in fact, the only thing I'm close to is joining a nunnery. Things seem so different now to when I was last single. Is it me? What should I be doing differently?

*T*wenty-first-century dating is brutal and I believe that online dating and social media are to blame. We have access to millions of potential partners at the touch of a button and it feels like this has led to people feeling less motivated to invest their time or effort into one person because they know that they can easily match another one within minutes. Since sex has become easier to get, love has become harder to find.

Sexual liberation and empowerment are utterly wonderful. I will forever be thankful to the women who campaigned in the sixties and whose actions meant that feminist causes became part of the public discussion, and to science, for giving people with wombs the chance to have more control over whether or not they get pregnant. However, now that men don't have to work particularly hard to get sex and they don't need to secure a partner in order to maintain an active sex life, they are much less likely to feel the need to be in a relationship. To be clear, I'm not saying there is anything at all wrong with women enjoying casual sex, nor am I reducing men to emotionless sex maniacs. Men want and need meaningful relationships too, but it is undeniable that the fuckboy types who want to shag and run or who continually enter into complicated situationships that never go anywhere have been enabled greatly, not only by the fact that women are now far more likely to have sex outside of an established relationship but also because there is an abundance of fresh, available women at their fingertips. Hook-up culture has impacted hugely on dating. I am not suggesting that we need to change anything, or that sexual liberation should reverse, but I think it's important to recognize that when you are messed around, or ghosted, or a man leads you into a situationship, it's not because you're doing something wrong or you're not good enough, it's just that the landscape has changed and you happened to run into a fuckboy (or several) whose pursuit of new vagina takes priority over his desire to settle down.

Having said all that, I think the first thing to remember is that dating should and can be fun. Dating should be all about the butterflies – those early connections, feeling good about yourself, enjoying the opportunity to get to know another human being and some excitement outside of your normal routine. Obviously, this book documents the shit you have to wade through before you get there, but don't let that make you forget that dating *should* be a pleasurable experience.

> **You will definitely encounter fuckboys on your journey, especially if you're on the apps, but you mustn't let them ruin the ride.**

Being open to the possibility of love means being open to the possibility of hurt, but it's worth it because when it's fun, it's so *fucking fun*, and you can always get over heartbreak. Let's look at the stuff you need to navigate at this stage so that you're going in with your eyes open.

Pink and red flags

The best way to avoid problems is to be really familiar with the pink and red flags covered in this book and to promise yourself that you will run from them when they appear. A red flag is something you should react to straight away, for example any of the signs of controlling behaviour, misogyny or being married or in a relationship. A pink flag is something that you should take note of; it's not necessarily something that would make you run immediately, but you should certainly sit up and take note. One pink flag in isolation may be nothing, but several pink flags add up to a red. For example, if they tell you that their ex-partner has a restraining order against them, that's a straight-up red flag. If they tell you that their ex-partner is having trouble letting go of their relationship, but they've now blocked them, that's a pink flag. If you see them wearing a wedding ring, that's a red flag. If they only ever seem able to communicate with you during the working day, that's a pink flag. On top of that, if they also say they have no social media, that's another pink flag. More than two pink flags are enough to equal a red. Don't become a flag collector. Take action.

That said, if you spend all your time dating being on high alert for flags, you will inevitably not be dating freely and truly as yourself; you will be in FBI mode (**Fuckboy Investigator**) and that will hamper your ability to enjoy the process. Red and pink flags will present themselves in time; your only job is to react to them if and when they do appear.

Gameplaying

The biggest lesson that I have learned is that to really find connections and to date with joy you have to be your genuine, authentic self. Every dating book I have ever read instructed me that I should be someone else in order to get the guy. Sherry Argov's *Why Men Love Bitches* was the first one I read. It was written in 2002, so it doesn't really apply to current times at all, but the whole premise is that in order to get a man to fall in love with you, you have to be a strong, independent, assertive woman (I approve of that part) who acts as though she is completely disinterested in the man she is pursuing. It tells you that you have to make a man chase you, and some choice advice includes: don't respond to calls for two hours; when he asks you out, say that you are busy but schedule for a later date; don't be too emotional; don't tell them how you feel, show them what they might lose instead. The advice works on the principle that if it comes too easily, men don't want it. And it kind of works. I think we have all been in that situation where someone we aren't interested in is super-keen and their enthusiasm becomes incredibly jarring. I've often wished that I could behave with men that I *do* like in the same way I do with the ones I don't – natural indifference seems to drive them crazy – but I find it impossible to fake it in the way *Why Men Love Bitches* recommends.

Dating advice geared towards men gives very similar tips, about being aloof and not replying to messages and not being too over-enthusiastic. So we're *all* being told the same thing – to act really cool, to pretend not to give a shit, to lie about having an active social life, to play games in order to get laid – and it's leading us into weird false dynamics with people we can never really get to know properly because we are constantly pretending to be bitches and bastards. Some of us aren't assertive; some of us are very full on; some of us wear our hearts on our sleeves; some of us can't cope with trying to act in ways that are completely counter-intuitive so, when we do, we come across as slightly unhinged. This outdated advice forces you to seek connection by being totally focused on yourself and your own behaviour rather than being able to relax and tune into the other person's.

> **And I don't actually think that *genuinely nice* men really like bitches.**

I think they like the chase as much as the rest of us, but I think it's more your self-titled 'alpha male' with narcissistic tendencies who tends to go after women they think don't want them. The nice guy is more likely to read the signs and think, 'I'm gutted but I don't want to push this woman's boundaries if she isn't interested.' It also creates a power struggle around who is in control, who likes who more, who can play the best game to win the other person over. Once power struggles come into play in relationships, you're already in a losing battle. Relationships should be the one safe space where you feel that you can relinquish power and surrender.

We start to find better connections when we are unapologetically ourselves. No façade, no tactical behaviour, no pretending to be anything other than who we are. Although not being too keen too soon is very important. Don't play games, but don't be *too* over-enthusiastic. Give a bit

Once **power struggles** come into play in relationships, you're already in a **losing battle.**

of chase, but also let them know you're interested. Get busy, even if that just means watching a series or reading a book with your phone on silent. That way, you are *genuinely* not replying for a while, rather than tactically trying to behave as if you don't like him.

We are taught by society and popular culture that to get a man you have to be a certain type of woman: feminine, submissive, fragile, strong, independent but in need of a masculine man, good in bed but a virgin, have Michelin-starred cooking skills but be slim, have no desire to go out and party, be well-groomed but 'natural'. And sometimes we find ourselves playing up to that. We play a character that we think men want us to be. When I was newly seeing or talking to a guy, my whole social media would suddenly be geared towards showing him that I was the woman for him. My Instagram would go from mainly pictures of my son to some kind of weird amateur cookery/exercise/glamour channel with memes and motivational quotes I knew he'd like thrown in for good measure.

All the posts would be carefully thought out to impress my love interest as much as possible. If he liked the gym, I'd be Instagramming every gym session – but not until the sweat was glistening seductively on my cleavage. And every man likes eating, so of course I'd photograph every stew and curry I made in an attempt to ensure that he knew I had mastered the skill of putting ingredients together and heating them. If he was into poetry, I'd whack a few deep poems up on my stories, like a poetry connoisseur. If he didn't like the picture or respond to the story, it would feel like a tragedy. Instead of replying to his texts, I'd be indirectly trying to get his attention on social media by altering all my hobbies and interests to make it seem like we had loads in common. It would have been much easier to just opt for men I had loads in common with.

Attempts to impress aren't just reserved for online antics. Many of us have gone above and beyond to try to wow people who are barely giving us the time of day. Things like getting tattoos or piercings because we know he is into tatted women, helping them to rewrite their CVs, or meal prepping twelve lunches for them. It's this need to show them how much better their lives could be with us around. We want to create dependency through fixing them or assisting them with their lives. We want to become useful and indispensable. We want to be a nurturing supportive mother replacement, often for zero reciprocity. We need to learn to nurture ourselves instead.

You are who you are, and you're not going to be too keen, or too shy, or too enthusiastic, or too loud, or too much, or too anything for the right person. Putting on a performance is hard work, and we only feel it's necessary when we don't love ourselves enough. You are good enough as you are. Think about the reasons why someone would be lucky to have *you*. There are definitely at least five. Write them down. Give yourself daily affirmations, tell yourself that you are fabulous, even when you don't fully feel it. Look in the mirror and tell yourself that you are enough and date with that in mind.

> **If they can't take us as we are, then we don't want them.**

First dates

First dates are exciting, nerve-wracking, anxiety-provoking. It could end up being the start of a lifelong romance or something you can turn into a hysterical story you dine out on for the next ten years. And if you're a woman on a date with a man, it could also be far worse than just a wild story. I discuss the safety aspects in Chapter 8, but if you happen to be going on a first date between reading this chapter and that one, let me just make it very clear – don't go to a man's house or invite him to yours if you've never met, even if you just want to sleep with him. It's unsafe, but also, even if he's a totally safe person, what if you suddenly get the ick? What if he is not what you expected in person? What if there is a weird energy or the chemistry is just off? Then you're stuck in an awkward situation that could have been avoided if you'd met for coffee first. Dinners are a bad idea, because it's hard to duck out early if things aren't great.

Then plan a proper date for next time (if you get to a second date without being ghosted, that is.)

If you do go for dinner or drinks, there is always the age-old question of who should pay. It's important to bear in mind that there are a lot of politics surrounding this issue. I'm going to tell you my personal view, but this is not a hard-and-fast rule. Lots of women prefer to split the bill; some may prefer to pay it all. But, for me, if a man does not offer to pay, I take it as a sign that he is not interested. I will always offer to split the bill, but if he doesn't decline my offer, we will be unlikely to have a second date. The gender pay gap does still exist, I'm more likely to incur expensive cab fares, given women's safety issues, whereas he can safely jump on a Tube, and it's likely to have cost me a hell of a lot more in beauty treatments in preparation for the date than it has for him to spray on a bit of aftershave. (Quick note: I obviously bang on about how we don't need to meet men's beauty expectations, and that we're good enough as we are, and so nobody *needs* to beautify themselves before a date, but I enjoy it and I want to get glammed up. That doesn't mean that you have to: all of this is subjective and not every woman is going to care about getting her hair done before a date.) Equally, it's important to say that even if the man has paid for dinner, he should not expect sex in return. I saw a poll on a male page on Insta recently that asked whether men felt that if they paid for dinner, that meant they were entitled to sex. Seventy-nine per cent said yes. The fact that the value of a woman's body and a glass of wine or a nice meal are equated is fucking wild. We don't owe them anything, no matter how much they've spent, how nice the restaurant is or how far they've travelled to get there.

It is common for men to try to bypass the first date entirely. Often, they will nonchalantly ask when you're going to cook for them, or they'll say, 'I'm not really a social kind of guy, I prefer chilling and getting to know

each other to noisy bars and restaurants.' No matter how he fran
he wants to have the first meeting in either his flat or yours, he pr
wants to have sex. So, if you're not looking for that straight away,
boundaries very firmly from the outset.

However, be prepared to be met with resistance when you set these
boundaries. Men often respond by making you feel foolish – they may
suggest that it's childish to be scared of a man coming over. Or they will
act as though they are offended if you mention that it's unsafe. Or they will
belittle you by making a joke about the fact that they will be able to control
themselves because you're not that hot. Or suggest that you are being wild
by thinking that no man can be around a woman without trying it on.

If their gaslighting is skilful enough, it might make you question
whether perhaps you are being a bit OTT. Let me reassure you: you're
not. But if they do manage to convince you that it's a good idea to invite
them over and that they won't try it on, there is a high chance that you'll
find yourself in a situation where things do become sexual.

> **The first date has to be in public. It's just not worth the risk.**

A good man will understand and will be patient and kind. He won't mock
you for setting boundaries, so set them loud and clear – it's a great way to
filter out potential dickheads. If you set boundaries and those boundaries
make them disappear, then that is a wonderful thing.

Deciding whether to have sex on the first night is another potential
hurdle. Most dating books aimed at heterosexual women say the same
thing – to avoid it – and some writers, such as Steve Harvey, in his
misogynistic book *Act Like a Lady, Think Like a Man*, suggest waiting
as long as ninety days. Many fuckboys will cruelly test women on their
attitude towards sex on a first date. They will make out that they are
open-minded and think nothing of two adults having sex when they
are both horny and into each other, but secretly they will be trying to
establish how easy it is to get you into bed, and if it happens too quickly,
you will have failed their wifeability test. This is utter scumbag behaviour,

but that doesn't take away from the feeling of being used or the shame that can come from realizing that you got played. So, not sleeping with a man on the first date can protect you from these types.

Many millions of marriages have started out with first-date sex, and men who don't have misogynistic views and double standards around women and sex simply don't judge us for it. However, in my experience, sometimes getting down and dirty very early on can kill the vibe. It can make something that had long-term potential into a casual hook-up, not because you've been judged, but because it often automatically means that the next time you see each other you will be meeting up for sex. It can divert the path of things. I also think that the build-up is sexy. Waiting creates desire, and in the meantime you become more confident and comfortable with each other so that when you do have sex, it's likely to be better. I don't think it's a good idea to announce that you're waiting or to tell the man that you have set a number of dates that have to happen before you will have sex with him. This can come across as immature and tactical, so it's better to make sure that you date in places where it's not easy for sex to happen until you're ready to do it. Saying 'Come to mine, but we're not having sex' doesn't often work; some men see it as a challenge. Also, don't do that thing where you purposely don't shave (if you're someone who removes body hair) in an attempt to stop yourself from having sex before you intend to; it doesn't work and your first time together is then ruined by the fact that you can't stop thinking about your bush. (FYI most men don't care about your bush – and if they do, they don't deserve access to it. Your pubes are your choice: if you're shaved and he complains that he prefers a bush, he can fuck off. And if you're unshaved and he complains about the amount of hair, he can also fuck off.)

Being ready should really be based on how you feel – do you like them? Fancy the shit out of them? Is your fanny fluttering at the thought of them? Are you having sex with them because you want to and not because you believe that you need to do it to ensure they stick around? Have sex because you want to cum, have sex because you love physical pleasure, have sex because you choose to for your own needs, but do not have sex for someone else's benefit or to make them want you – it will not end well.

Go into first dates wondering whether *you* will like *them* rather than the other way around. And make sure that you really do like *them* rather than the fantasy version you might be projecting. Ask yourself if the two of you really are a good match or is it because they're six foot three? Are they listening to you and showing an interest in your life and your opinions? Do they get your jokes? Are you on the same wavelength? Do you feel at ease in their company? Focus on that stuff, *not* on whether they are into you and what you can do to make them like you.

Infatuation

If you are someone who finds that they get a bit obsessed by the people they are seeing, then I would really recommend reading up on limerence. 'Limerence' is a term coined by psychologist Dorothy Tennov to describe a state of mind that takes over when some people have a crush. It is heavily connected to attachment theory and tends to be experienced by people with insecure attachments. Limerence often looks something like this: you meet someone who you find extremely attractive and from that moment on they take over your mind and become your limerent object. You become obsessed by them, ruminating about them all day. You try not to, but frequent intrusive thoughts about them keep entering your head. You become anxious, especially if there is a delay in messaging or they don't contact you straight after a date. Everything becomes about them; if there was a song playing when you first got in their car, you play it over and over. If they mentioned that they love *EastEnders*, you begin watching it religiously. This should not be mistaken for love – love involves wanting to care for the other person; limerence is more about just having them, no matter what. People in limerence overlook all red flags; they even overlook whether they have anything in common with the other person.

Limerence causes us to become infatuated and to look for signs and hidden clues that the other person feels the same way. You attach meaning to tiny, insignificant things to prove to yourself that they secretly desire you. You will experience a strong fear of rejection that makes you panic when you don't hear from them for a few hours. But rejection won't put you off. It will make the limerence more intense. You completely lose yourself and it begins to take over your life. Your world revolves entirely around them. If the opportunity to see them arises, you find that you would cancel attending your mum's birthday dinner just to be with them for an hour. You are spurred on by the fact that they are unattainable; their ambivalence and indifference drive you crazy, but it doesn't put you off. It makes you want to give them all the benefits of a relationship so that they see how indispensable you are.

There are three ways in which limerence can end. First, eventually, the other person may reciprocate your feelings and you end up in a mutually loving relationship. This is unlikely though as you will probably have already scared them off with your intensity. Second, you can cut them out completely and **block, delete and move on**: you can force it to end by telling yourself that you are in a state of limerence and that none of these feelings are based on anything other than your own attachment style. Third, you end up transferring your desires to someone else and the object of your limerence changes. It really is worth reading more on this if you recognize these behaviours in yourself. They cause us to end up giving everything to the wrong people for the wrong reasons.

Ghosting

Being ghosted is hellish. We've all been there: when you've been chatting to someone for a while, or you've had a couple of dates, maybe even more, and you thought things were going well, but then a day goes by and you don't hear back from them. And then another day. And maybe another. At this point your stomach sinks and your head goes into hurricane mode: you can't think about anything else but them, you become obsessed with checking your phone and their social media for clues as to what has happened. You check their recent Insta pictures to see if there are any RIP messages from their friends, secretly hoping that death is the reason for their silence, not the fact that they've lost interest. The hardest thing is deciding whether to reach out. Should I double text, even though I sent the last message and I've been left on read? Maybe they think I've gone off them and if I don't get in touch, it might ruin things? Maybe I said something that I need to apologize for? Maybe they are having a mental breakdown and need support? Maybe they lost their phone? Maybe I don't even give a fuck whether texting makes me look like a dick? Or maybe texting will put them off because they are testing me to see how cool I can be? It's a stressful nightmare.

The way I see it is this: if communication suddenly changes without explanation and you can *feel* the shift and your gut is telling you that things are off, they probably are. No message is a message. If contacting someone is going to put them off, then they weren't interested in the first place. Reaching out might make you feel bad because you might get a shit response, or no response, but is that any worse than spending the next week feeling confused about what has happened? If you can accept that you've been ghosted and you can take it on the chin and close that chapter without feeling conflicted, then don't text them. But if you feel like you want answers and you can't settle until you try one last time, then be my guest. But if you are met with silence or a one-word answer, then give up. It's not worth your energy. The universe did you a favour: it wasn't meant to be.

If you find out that you definitely have been ghosted, try not to internalize this as meaning that there is something wrong with you. There are a million reasons why someone might ghost that have nothing to do with you. They might have secretly been in a relationship all along; they might be suffering from overwhelming anxiety; they might have run out of money and be too embarrassed to tell you that they can't go out; they might have decided that you're not a great match and not know how to tell you; they might have unexpectedly reconnected with their ex; maybe they got the ick. You don't need to know why they've ghosted in order to be able to move on. You just have to accept that, for whatever reason, they didn't tell you why they no longer wanted to pursue things with you. That's it. There is no reason to soul-search about it. Even if the reason was that they have gone off you, that doesn't mean that there is something wrong with you. It just means you weren't for them, and that's okay. Not everyone we talk to or go on a date with is a potential partner. They're not a prize, they're not the only person for you and they don't set the bar for how other people will feel about you.

Ghosting is hurtful and cruel. It's a horrible way to treat someone else and it says a lot about the frame of mind of the ghoster. So be aware of zombies who return to haunt you. A zombie is a ghoster who comes back from the dead, usually with a 'Hey, stranger!' message and no acknowledgement of the fact that they disappeared. When you tell a zombie that you thought they had died they will give you a sob story or a ridiculous excuse like 'You probably won't even believe this, but my phone fell into a volcano and I lost all my numbers.' It's up to you to decide whether their explanation is sufficient for you to give it another go. But ghosters are often repeat offenders, so only resume things if you know that them going AWOL again is not going to devastate you.

If they don't disappear completely but pop up every now and again, they may be breadcrumbing. Breadcrumbing is when someone is not interested in you enough to give you their time or attention but they want to keep you around, so they keep dropping crumbs and getting in touch sporadically to hold you there. There are several reasons why someone might do this: either they're a narcissistic fuckboy and it feeds their ego; or they're a no-labels fuckboy who only contacts you for sex; or they want to ensure that the next time they want sex, you'll be around; or they're into someone else but they want options in case it doesn't work out. The thing about breadcrumbers and zombies is that they seem to have some kind of magical radar that tells them exactly when to get in touch. It always seems to happen just as you have stopped thinking about them, or just as you have told yourself that you need to let this one go, or just as you are feeling a bit lonely and fragile. The key is to make sure that you don't place meaning on sporadic interactions. We often convince ourselves that the fact that they keep coming back means that they must have deep feelings for us and they just cannot let us go, even though their behaviour is really showing us that their feelings are minimal.

> If someone is interested, then they will be consistent.

They will be in touch regularly because they want to be, and they will make plans because they will want to see you. You won't have to beg them to pay you more attention or to stay in contact more frequently. You won't feel anxious for days on end, wondering where they are and where you stand, you won't only hear from them sporadically when they feel like it. You will know that they are interested and keen because they will show you through their actions.

Should I text them?

Most of us will have been in the situation where we want to send a message to someone who has been ignoring us, or treating us badly, to ask them what's going on or why they have behaved in a particular way. We know they're a fuckperson, we know deep down that our best bet would be to **block, delete and move on**. Our guts are telling us not to send the message because we already know the answer, but we feel compelled to send it anyway. Some small glimmer of hope that they have been waiting for us to text all along will compel us to hit send, and then we regret it instantly when they reply with something upsetting or they don't reply at all. In order to prevent people from sending regrettable texts, I do a feature on my Instagram called Fuckboy Replies, where my followers send a text to me instead of sending it to their fuckperson. I then reply to it in the style of a fuckperson, or as myself with my own thoughts. The replies are often brutal and blunt – because sometimes we need a bit of tough love to remind us to fix up.

Here are some examples that might help you think twice about sending a text to a fuckboy:

Why did you tell me that you didn't want a relationship, but now you are in one with her? Was I not good enough for you?

Asking this kind of question is self-harm. I get an abundance of questions like this whenever I do Fuckboy Replies, and I don't see how any good can come from asking it. He wanted a relationship with her, not you. It's as simple as that. Maybe he finds her more attractive or easier to get along with. Is that what you want to hear from him? That he finds someone else more appealing than you? Or maybe it's because he realized that you weren't going to take his shit, so he went for someone who would. Or perhaps it's because you were taking too much of his shit and he lost respect for you. Before asking a question like this, think about why you are asking it. He doesn't owe you an explanation. He told you that he didn't want a relationship with you, but you stuck around, hoping that he would change his mind, and instead he gave the relationship you wanted to someone else. This is not because you did anything wrong (although if you gave him relationship benefits without him reciprocating your energy, then you need to learn from this), it's not because you aren't good enough, or that you are less worthy or less beautiful than his current girlfriend. You just weren't a match for him. He didn't want a relationship with you, that's it: no soul-searching needed. **Block, delete, move on**.

Why do you come over whenever I text you, but you never text me first or initiate meeting up?

Because he's not that into you beyond sex. He doesn't think about you much day to day, but when you text him with an offer of casual vagina he thinks, 'Cool! Why not?' He likes having sex with you, but he doesn't want anything beyond that. Another variation of this one that often comes up is: *Why do you only contact me when you're drunk or high, or after nights out?*, and the answer is very similar. He sees you as a booty call. Convenient sex when he's horny and high. Stop giving it to him! You are being treated casually by someone who you have caught feelings for. Don't question why he treats you casually, question why you are compromising your own needs to keep him around. Set your boundaries, refuse to meet up for sex, suggest dates instead, put your phone on silent at night so that you don't jump out of bed for his booty calls. If that puts him off, then you have successfully filtered out someone who was making you unhappy.

I still hate you for how you treated me, but I miss you.

Do you miss him, or do you miss the familiarity of his chaos? Do you miss the self-harm element of his mistreatment of you, the way it confirmed to you that your negative beliefs about yourself were true? Are you bonded to him because of the trauma he put you through? Maybe you miss him because there were times when he made you feel amazing, but is it worth risking the bad stuff for the glimmer of good? You have done so well to be out of this and reaching out because you are having a low moment will rewind your progress. The likelihood is that he hasn't changed and he probably won't. He showed up in your relationship as his true self, and that guy made you feel like shit. You're going to miss him, but that doesn't mean you should contact him. It means you need to channel it into something else. Write out a list of negatives, remind yourself of all the bad times. Ride it out and don't look back.

The most important thing Fuckboy Replies has taught me is that I never want to be a 'paragraph girl' again. I have spent hours carefully constructing deeply emotional, heartfelt paragraphs to men in the hope that my woes will tug at their heartstrings, but I now realize that most men don't even read them. They see a big paragraph coming through and think, 'This is a fucking headache,' and it doesn't serve to make them love you or want you, it just confirms that dating you is pure stress and not worth the hassle. This is not to say that you don't have the right to pour your heart out and say how you truly feel, it's just that long essays to men who haven't been giving you time, effort or commitment are never going to achieve what you want them to achieve. Write it out in notes to get it off your chest and be done with it.

The ick

The ick is one of the most horrible things to happen when you are dating someone or, even worse, when you are in a relationship with them. 'The ick' is the term used to describe that feeling of being instantly and often inexplicably turned off by someone you were once turned on by. It can be for a very rational reason, like discovering that they have a toenail collection, or it can be for something so incredibly irrational that you begin to think there's something wrong with you, like them dropping their hat accidentally. From the moment the ick hits, it feels like you can't even look at them any more. Everything they do becomes super-irritating; things that you once found cute are now fucking grossing you out. You wince when they try to kiss you and you can't bear the sound of them chewing.

> Once the ick hits, it is very hard to backtrack from it and it tends to get progressively worse.

The ick is horrible because quite often you don't want to experience this shift. This is someone you liked, someone you could have seen a future with and they haven't actually done anything wrong, so you get trapped into feeling like a total bitch and not wanting to hurt them or lose them, but needing to end it because the sound of their breathing makes you want to cut your ears off. I believe that the ick is your gut's way of telling you that something is off and our guts are in-built life guides, danger detectors. For whatever reason, we're not supposed to be with the people we get the ick with; we just need to trust our gut.

Before you give them the elbow, you need to check yourself to make sure that it's definitely the ick and not self-sabotage. I have been guilty of the latter on several occasions. Things will be going well, the guy seems lovely and is reciprocating my energy and I will suddenly panic that it all appears to be too good to be true. So I start searching for things that don't feel right and begin over-analysing tiny things that could potentially be problematic in the future. I'll start thinking, 'Well, he's not originally from London, so what's going to happen in five years' time if he wants to move back home? Better end it now before I get hurt.' Sometimes we are so fearful of rejection and so used to having to protect ourselves from hurt we begin to invent reasons why we don't like them in our heads so that if they do end up disappearing, or being awful, we can say we never liked them anyway. Is it the ick or is it a defence mechanism?

The other traumatic thing about having experienced the ick is the knowledge that someone has probably felt it with us before. We've probably been thinking that a guy is loving our company and all the while he's sitting there wanting to vomit because of the way we're playing with our hair. Some of those times when we've been ghosted, or when they've dumped us out of the blue, have probably resulted from them feeling the ick with us. It's a horrible thought, but it's not one we should take personally. It can happen with the sexiest, most amazing people for no apparent reason. It's not you, it's the ick.

Trust your gut

When everyone tells you to rely on your gut, but the overriding feelings coming from the pit of your stomach are a constant fizzy mess and you feel like something bad is happening all the time, it's a complete headfuck. But that's exactly how you can tell the difference between gut instinct and anxiety. Anxiety is relentless; it leaves you uncertain and worried about things that might never happen. It's based on a hypothetical rather than on anything concrete. Gut instinct is occasional

GUT INSTINCT IS

REAL

AND IT'S

POWERFUL

AND WE SHOULD

TRUST IT

and is a much more certain feeling. Gut instinct is real and it's powerful and we should trust it. There is a big difference between the physiological things that happen when you are experiencing generalized anxiety (a loss of appetite, inability to sleep, raised heart rate, a constant sick feeling, worrying about future things that you have been given no reason to worry about) and the very calm and knowing feeling that you experience when it's your gut instinct.

For example, if you are newly speaking to someone and anxiety is raging, you might be constantly worrying about what could go wrong. Your brain might create fifty different scenarios in which they might hurt you and thoughts of each scenario avalanche into a billion other thoughts about not being good enough or about something going wrong. But, deep down, you know, when you rationalize things and take stock of their actual behaviour, that they have done nothing to cause this and that your brain is just running wild. That is very different to being presented with a specific situation that makes you go, 'Oh, hold up, this is something that has made me feel really uneasy.' Female intuition is a real thing, an evolutionary tool that we developed to protect our babies. Research has shown that while all humans have intuition, women's intuition is stronger than men's.[8] Sometimes it's hard to trust our guts because we are taught that logic prevails, that a gut feeling can't be right without evidence, that women are 'crazy' and 'over-emotional' and that we should listen to men's logic over women's feelings. But we must learn to trust that feeling – always. However, even when you have evidence as well as gut instinct, it is very easy to be thrown off track by gaslighting. You can show a man a screenshot of a conversation with a woman and they will tell you you've gone crazy and that that's not even a woman. We have to stand firm.

8   Austin, Ashleigh. 'Science confirms women's intuition is a real thing'. *New York Post*, 16 June 2017. https://nypost.com/2017/06/16/science-confirms-womens-intuition-is-a-real-thing

Single parents

Single parenting adds an entirely new dimension of complexity to dating life. How hard it is will depend on what your support network is like and whether the man you've had kids with is being controlling and judgemental about you moving on. Everybody's ability to have child-free time differs. If you only have child-free time every other weekend or less, it can really impact on being able to build momentum with people. And once you do start talking, you have to think far more carefully about letting them know where you live. It should go without saying that you should not invite men you barely know to your house while your child or children are there, even if they've gone to bed. It is also inadvisable to state that you are a single parent on your profile; however, it is important to let them know early on in the conversation – just drop it in when they ask what your plans are this week. Many women have found that guys have disappeared and ghosted them as soon as they find out they have children, which can make it feel like an affliction – but it's not, it's a lucky escape.

Lots of things can make it feel like you have become less attractive after becoming a single parent, for example changes to your body, the daily hardcore parenting life, having less time for self-care, not to mention society's perception of single mothers and your total inability to be spontaneous. But there is nothing unattractive about a person who can single-handedly raise another human. It's not unsexy either; in fact, 'MILF' is the second-most-searched term, according to Pornhub. I find this troubling, because while I don't want to be sexually objectified and fetishized for being mature and maternal, when I first read it I felt quite encouraged about the fact that I'm still hot. Then I wanted to punch myself.

It is more than possible to find great partners who will make an amazing addition to you and your child or children's lives. It is possible to find whatever you are looking for. We just have to date with our children in mind. They are even more motivation to run from red flags.

EVER FORCE IT.

SETTLE.

LOWER YOUR STANDARDS.

IGNORE RED FLAGS.

Enjoy the ride

It is okay to go on twenty dates with twenty different people and not find one who you want to settle down with. You are a unique individual and to find another human you are completely compatible with you have to weed through a lot of non-starters first. But you do not have to try to make it work with everyone you meet. Don't ever force it. Don't change your personality or your interests in order to make it work. Don't dampen your intelligence. Don't downplay your wit. Don't settle. Don't see being in a relationship as your goal. Don't lower your standards. Don't ignore incompatibilities. Don't give up your precious single days until you find the right one. Don't sacrifice your own needs to keep, or get, a partner. Don't date when your self-esteem is low. Don't ignore red flags. Don't take rejection personally. Remember that if it was meant to be, it would have been. We get more than one soulmate, so make the journey to finding them all a fun one.

Remember that if it was meant to be, it would have been.

Chapter 7:

Is he worth disturbing your pH for?

I need to tell you about this prick I met on Hinge. I didn't even really want him to come over, but it was a Saturday night and my two best friends were out with their partners and I was feeling needy. We went out for the first time about a month ago after talking for ages, but he messed me around after our first date. Not replying to messages, cancelling our second date at the last minute, all that shit. I was still very much interested in him, but because I was feeling weird about his behaviour I wanted to stand my ground. I caved when he caught me at the wrong moment and offered to come over with a bottle of wine. I told myself that I wasn't going to sleep with him, but I shaved just in case. Two hours and two bottles of wine later and we were in bed. The sex was average: not terrible, barely any foreplay, and I didn't cum. He left at 4 a.m., which I was actually thankful for. It's now Thursday and I swear to God, I've got BV, thrush and a fucking UTI. AND I haven't heard from him since. Can you please invent some way of taking back sex? I HATE this feeling.

f I could invent an app where we could take back our regrettable sex, I would be the richest woman in the world. I'm working on it but, in the meantime, all we can do is treat the thrush and make sure we never have sex with them again. Deciding whether or not to sleep with somebody is something we should really give some thought to, to prevent those potential regrets, whether it's with your ex, someone you've been on a few dates with or just some random you've met on the apps. In Chapter 6 I talked about whether to have sex on a first date, but I think it's also important to give consideration to how you might feel about having any sex that's outside of an established relationship. So when I say 'casual sex', I don't necessarily mean one-night stands; I'm referring to any sex that you have before the conversation around exclusivity and where things are going. In that weird period after you've been on a few dates but before you've had the conversation, it can feel perfectly natural and reasonable to start sleeping with each other. But I've been in that situation where I've had sex with a guy, thinking that the dates and everything would continue as normal, only to discover that afterwards I've become nothing more than a booty call in his eyes, and that's not what I'd wanted.

As far as I'm concerned, there is no debate to be had around whether it's acceptable for women to have casual sex. It is absolutely 100 per cent okay if you enjoy it, and it is nothing to be judged or frowned upon. We have been made to think it's not okay by religion, culture and governments who sought to control society and birth rates, and misogyny has continued those narratives. But we have made some progress since then and we now have the means to prevent pregnancy and infection. You do not have to be in a relationship to be able to enjoy safe sex. However, you do have to know whether you are someone who can handle casual sex. If you cannot handle being treated casually

by someone you are sleeping with, then you cannot handle casual sex, and the honest truth is that many women can't. It's important to note that 'casually' does not mean disrespectfully: casual sex should still be respectful, the casual part simply refers to how often you speak to them in between and the fact that it's outside of an established relationship.

To figure out if you're a person who can have casual sex, think about the reasons why you are doing it. If you are only having sex because all your mates are doing it and you want to fit in, then you cannot handle casual sex. If the person you want doesn't want to commit to you and you are only having sex with them to keep them in your life, then you cannot handle casual sex. If you are only having sex for validation and attention but it leaves you unfulfilled and craving more, then you cannot handle casual sex. If you are always left feeling lonely and regretful afterwards, then you cannot handle casual sex.

On the other hand, if you are making choices about having intimacy and enjoying sexual pleasure and feeling fantastic afterwards, regardless of whether they call you the next day, then you can handle casual sex.

My non-scientific unofficial studies into my own sex life and that of my friends have shown me that often, after three sex sessions with the same person, we want to ask, 'What are we?', even if we started off casual, and even if we don't actually like them or have that much in common with them. Then we end up in situationships or become infatuated with an absolute bell-end, not because he's the greatest guy in the world, but because we got attached to the sex. Which is precisely why we should try to establish whether we can handle casual before jumping fanny first into one of those scenarios. We also need to look at those scenarios where we know that he's no good for us but we tell ourselves that the sex is so good that it's worth sticking around.

> **Sometimes we convince ourselves that the sex is good because that's the only time he's giving us his full attention.**

I had a toxic ex I used to use this excuse about: I told my mates that I couldn't give him up because the sex was so good. But when I look back on it, it wasn't really that great. He wasn't asking me what I liked or centring the event around what worked for me. It was okay sex, not great sex, but I interpreted it as great because it was the only time when he would tell me how beautiful I was and how much he loved being with me and how his dick was mine. (I later found out that it was definitely not mine. It belonged to the community.) It was the one time when I felt important and when he wasn't distracted by other, more exciting things in his life. It wasn't even the sex that turned me on, it was falling asleep in his arms afterwards.

When you strip it all back – the attention, the validation, the intimacy, the compliments ... is it really that great? Is he making your toes curl? Are you tingling all over? Are you genuinely orgasming because of the intense pleasure and desire he is making you feel? Or are you just hanging on to the bare minimum and setting the sex bar low because you don't know any different, or because you don't feel that you deserve more? Is he really good in bed or is he just making you feel wanted for a brief moment?

And if he is knocking your socks off and giving you multiple orgasms but is ruining your life or fucking up your head outside of the bedroom, then why are you prioritizing good sex over your emotional wellbeing? Why are you setting the bar so low for yourself that you would accept pain and problems for the sake of a decent fuck? We have got to remember that a healthy relationship and good sex aren't mutually exclusive. You can have both. But it's harder to find a healthy relationship when you are dedicating your whole heart to someone who is toxic to you. Sticking around in a relationship or situationship that harms your peace is a waste of your one short life. Get yourself a man who doesn't disrupt your life or your pH balance.

It's perfectly okay to not be able to handle a more casual arrangement, and there's no shame in preferring things to be no-strings. But, as women, we have a lot more to consider than men. If a pregnancy happened, it would be a far greater burden for us to bear. I think it's important to talk about abortion here, as it is something that many people experience. Abortion is a valid choice, but it impacts on everybody differently. Some people experience nothing but relief while others experience guilt and regret; some experience a myriad of emotions. There is no right way to feel. It is the pregnant woman's choice entirely and we should not feel pressured or forced into making a decision that doesn't feel right for us and our body. The people we are sleeping with should support us in whatever choice we make and we should expect them to accompany us to appointments, if that's what we want. However, you do not have to tell them about the pregnancy if that would make the experience more difficult, or even dangerous, and you are not obliged to tell future partners that you have had an abortion in the past. It's nobody's business but yours. (@doposupport is a great resource on Instagram for people who require holistic support before, during and after an abortion.)

Sexually transmitted infections are another factor to consider, and even if we don't catch an STI, there is always the risk that we will end up with an itchy, uncomfortable vagina for days after sex. Cystitis after good sex is one thing, but after mediocre sex where you barely felt a tingle it's a fucking tragedy. And if you're having sex with men, then there's about a 50 per cent chance that the casual sex you do have is going to be mediocre, bad or orgasmless.

The orgasm gap

Sex is different for men and women. I don't know how sex feels for men – I wish I did. I would love to know what the sensation is when a penis enters a vagina. It must be magical. I feel like it must be off-the-charts fantastic, since so many of them will lie for weeks to get laid, beg for it and create double or even triple lives to get it. I imagine that it must feel a bit like when you get a head massage and it makes you tingle all over, but times ten and all concentrated in the tip of their dick.

I've asked many male friends what sex feels like, and it seems that the only answer they can give is 'warm, wet, tight and different every time'. They don't seem to be able to convey the actual sensation of the penis entry; they only seem to be capable of describing the feeling of a vagina.

I put up a question box on Instagram in my quest to find out. The vast majority of answers were variations of 'warm', 'wet' and 'soft'. Some were a little more poetic, like the guy who wrote, 'Like marshmallows covered in olive oil in a velvet pouch,' which sounds like a sticky mess to me. Many said that it felt like pressure relief. 'Like coming home,' said another. One chap said it was like 'the feeling of running your tongue on the roof of your mouth but less sensitive'. Try it. Now spend the rest of the day wondering why they are out here ruining lives for that shit.

I'm not suggesting that sex doesn't feel amazing for women. It's supposed to feel amazing, plus, we have the benefit of our orgasms lasting longer and of being able to have multiple orgasms. There is a myth that the clitoris contains around twice as many nerve endings as the penis but, according to @thesexdoctor Karen Gurney, it's around the same amount; they are just condensed into a much smaller space. But despite our orgasmic abilities, you simply don't see women behaving in the desperate way men do around sex. Perhaps it's because men are almost guaranteed to experience something wonderful every time, while it's Russian roulette for us. What's the point in paying for sex, or leading a double life, when there's more chance of getting a scratched urethra than an orgasm?

In my poll on Instagram, responded to by over 20,000 women, 84 per cent said they had faked an orgasm, 69 per cent said that they had faked orgasms many times and 46 per cent said that they have faked more orgasms than they've had real ones. This is ridiculous, but it is ridiculousness that I have participated in. I didn't start having good sex until my mid-thirties. As far as I was concerned, sex was a pursuit to make men like me. It was not about my pleasure; it was about theirs. I knew that sex was supposed to feel good, but because I hadn't ever really experienced any pleasure from being penetrated, I believed that there was something wrong with me. I wasn't capable of physically enjoying sex, so I gave up on the idea of having sex that felt good to me. Friends would talk to me about the amazing sex they were having and I would chime in with accounts of how great my man was in bed, even though I would have to wait until he'd fallen asleep to make myself cum. I would watch porn where women went wild at the mere touch of their vulva and I'd become concerned about what was wrong with me. I'd read *Cosmo* articles about the best positions for sex and, when I tried them, I'd find that they all hurt equally and none of them did much. I thought I was broken and couldn't understand why every other woman was so easily orgasmic. Some are – some highly blessed women really do feel intense pleasure without much effort – but it took me a long time to realize that they are the minority and that I was experiencing sex in much the same way as the vast majority of heterosexual women. Seventy-three per cent of respondents reported that they could not orgasm from penis-in-vagina penetration. Yet this is seen as the *pièce de résistance*, the main event, the holy grail. Which is madness, considering that it only works for 27 per cent of us. If only 27 per cent of men could cum through penetration alone, penetration would be off the table. You'd see it in niche porn movies and it would never be featured in mainstream media. The predominant sex narrative is centred around what works for men, and that is an absolute tragedy for heterosexual women.

Women who have sex with women don't experience the same issues around sex as heterosexual women. There is no orgasm gap for lesbians.

This throws out the whole 'it's harder for women to cum' theory. We're perfectly capable of achieving orgasm; men are just failing to bring us to that point. It may not be quite as simple as it is for men, but our orgasms are easily achievable under the right conditions. I don't mean just having your clitoris stimulated correctly – it goes far deeper than that. He could be rubbing your clit like a boss, but if your mind is not in the right place because you are worried about how you feel, look or smell, or you are having flashes of guilt because you are worried that you shouldn't be doing this, or you are concerned about what he is thinking, or whether he is getting bored, or whether he will respect you in the morning, or you can't stop thinking about some random task that you forgot to get done, like paying your council tax, then it's just not going to happen. This is why I wonder about what the sensation must be for men, because though it feels great for us under the right circumstances, it does take a while to warm up to it. Our brains have to be in the right headspace. Maybe it's because men have been granted the ability to have sex freely and without worrying about being called slags or being respected less. We have been taught that sex isn't really for us, that it's a transactional tool to secure relationships and that we may be considered sluts if we have too much of it.

Yet it's definitely more than the physical sensation that drives men to lie, cheat and manipulate for sex. I believe it's the sense of conquering and proving their masculinity through the power of the penis. Society has long told men that the ability to fuck as many women as possible is an achievement and proof of their manliness. This is evidenced by that subsection of men who subscribe to the pick-up artist ideology and spend vast amounts of time learning how to fuck as many women as possible, often through manipulative and violent techniques. Their whole reason for living appears to be based on how many women they can sleep with, and they take pride in discussing it at length on weird forums or in YouTube videos. Men have been afforded a licence to go forth and shag as many people as they want, safe in the knowledge that they will be applauded for their prowess. And certain that they have a 90 per cent chance of ejaculating every time. We have not been granted the same licence.

> **We have quite literally been fucked over when it comes to sex.**

This all started because men run the world. I don't know how they managed that one either – that's a whole other conversation – but there are a number of factors that contribute to all of this.

Love your vulva

As women, we are not educated enough about our anatomy. Most women call their whole genital area a vagina; the word 'vulva' is barely used. I used to find the word 'vagina' cringey and embarrassing. I hated saying it because it sounds so clinical and gynaecological – and 'vulva' sounds like a family car. 'Pussy' or 'fanny' were my chosen terms. (Although 'pussy' also makes me cringe – I can't say it unless I'm sexting – and 'fanny' makes it sound like an elderly aunt. 'Minge' sounds like an angry gremlin and 'muff' sounds like something you warm your ears with.) I really struggle to find a term that sits right with me, and that tells us so much about how women's sexuality has been framed. Many adult women refer to their vulva and vagina as their 'privates', or simply 'down there'. Do you know any men who call their dick their 'privates' or 'down there'? I'll wait . . . We need to be teaching our children this stuff in the same way we teach them about their elbows and their knees. It is empowering for them to know the real terminology. It also helps in terms of safeguarding, as a child is able to disclose sexual abuse much more easily if they are comfortable using language about their own bodies. Your daughter should know that she has a vulva, not a 'minnie' or a 'moo'.

I was in my thirties when I learned that the clitoris isn't a little solitary button, that it is in fact just the tip of the iceberg. If you don't know what the whole clitoral structure looks like, have a quick Google. The bulbs sit inside, up near your urethra, and it is thought that the reason why some women can cum from penetration alone is because their bulbs are larger – your g-spot is basically your internal clitoris – so it's still essentially the clit that is making them cum. The reason it looks like a penis and a pair of balls is because we all start out as female. We all have the clitoris structure in utero, but some will turn into penises while others remain mainly an internal organ. Having sex with a woman without touching her clitoris is like having sex with a man without touching his penis. It's mind-blowing that it's such a neglected body part. It's always a good idea to get to know your clitoris. Think of the tip as the face of a clock and figure out what time is your go-to place for stimulation – three, five thirty, twelve? What amount of pressure do you like? Communicate that with partners and take control of your own pleasure.

We should be taught about our genitalia in detail, from the labia to the urethra. And we must be encouraged to look at them with a mirror so that we are comfortable and familiar with ourselves.

> **How can we expect to orgasm when we have no idea what we are working with or when we feel ashamed by how it looks?**

Vulva shaming is a thing; far too many people don't believe that their vulva and labia look attractive. Long or short, fat or thin, wrinkled or tight, brown or black, pink, purple or red, flappy or tucked – it is all normal. Every vulva looks different. Some labia are long on one side and short on the other; some clits are really big, some are tiny. None is more or less attractive than the other. The sooner we get really in tune with, and accepting of, our vulva and our vagina, the sooner we will start having better sex.

Grab a mirror right now and introduce yourself to your vulva (unless you're on a train or at work). The first time I did this I was like, *Woah*, but it made me feel so much more confident and sure of myself. As weird as this sounds, befriending your vagina and vulva is really important. When you think of your clit and your labia as your little mates who you need to love and care for, it makes a difference. Think about your poor clitoris, whose sole purpose in life is to give you thrills, and how she feels when she is sitting there being completely neglected. Imagine her excitement when you bring a visitor over to see her and her heartbreak when she is completely ignored. Think about your innocent little labia, just sitting there, chilling out, living her best labia life, feeling great, until you come along and tell her that she's ugly and that you're embarrassed by her. Treat your vulva as you would treat a friend – you wouldn't tell your friend that she was ugly compared to your other friends, so don't do it to your vulva. Your vulva is unique to you, and I guarantee you that it is beautiful (check out @the.vulva.gallery on Instagram to see an array of vulvas and how different they all look). Learn about her and care for her as if she's your best mate. It really helps.

Did I cum yet?

We are often unclear about where orgasms come from, what they are supposed to feel like and whether we've even had one if there is no squirting. I regularly get messages from women that say something along the lines of 'I don't think I have ever had an orgasm. I get a nice feeling and a climax when I masturbate, but I have never cum.' Cumming and orgasming are the same thing; the words are used interchangeably. You can squirt without having an orgasm, and you can have an orgasm without squirting. Many women do not squirt naturally, although they say that every woman is capable of it and there are lots of guides online that promise to show you how. Sadly, some women are embarrassed by squirting while others are embarrassed by not being able to squirt. It's become just another way that men can make us feel inadequate in bed. The song 'WAP' (wet ass pussy) by Cardi B and Megan Thee Stallion was seen by some as a majorly empowering chart-topper, but it also led to many ill-informed tweets and memes by men suggesting that WAP was caused by vaginal infection or that it was an undesirable trait because of the cleaning involved afterwards. I have received a ton of messages over the years from women who feel worried about their own vaginal wetness and whether it was 'too much' or off-putting to partners. Most advice says to just embrace it, but that becomes harder to do when you are sleeping with men who complain about having to change the sheets or who make you feel weird for being 'too' wet, which is exactly why we shouldn't sleep with those men. DAP (dry ass pussy) is also something that affects many women. Vaginal dryness is normal. It can be caused by mood, menstrual cycles, antidepressants, antihistamines, dehydration, the menopause, pregnancy/post-partum and smoking. I've had as many messages from women who are worried about vaginal dryness as I've had from women who are worried about vaginal wetness. The only reason it's not good to have DAP is because it can make sex feel painful and uncomfortable for us.

Lube needs to be normalized.

There is absolutely no shame in using it and it is important to bring it into the bedroom if WAP isn't occurring naturally, or even if it is (you may also wish to look into vaginal moisturizers). Either way, both situations are normal, and neither should carry any shame or embarrassment. It is important to remember that vaginal lubrication is not an indication of how turned on you are. You can be dry while mega turned on, and super wet while feeling nothing at all.

Orgasms occur on a spectrum too: you can have toe-curling, all-over-tingling, out-of-body experiences or you can have little fizzles of pleasure. You can build up all the way to what feels like it's going to be a great orgasm and then you can lose it at the last minute and feel barely anything, like a failed sneeze. You can have clitoral orgasms, nipple orgasms, anal orgasms, cervical orgasms – even blended orgasms, where you have more than one form of orgasm at the same time.

Masturbation is the key. The importance of learning about your own body and what works for you cannot be overstated. Masturbation is another thing that can be loaded with shame and feelings of disgust but, at its core, masturbation is a form of self-care.

If you know how to make yourself climax, then it will be far easier to explain to someone else how to make you cum. Although, having said that, many women will find that they can orgasm easily by themselves but never with anyone else present, for all the reasons we are exploring here. Masturbating during sex is the only way that a lot of women can cum during penetration and there should be no shame in doing it. Experiment, explore and figure out what works for you, and don't be afraid to vocalize it in the bedroom. Get to know yourself first. Try watching ethical porn, reading erotica, experimenting with toys. Play with your sexuality. Embrace and explore things that make your fanny flutter. @am.appointment on Instagram is an excellent page to follow for lots of masturbation tips.

However, at the same time, remember that orgasms are not the be all and end all: we can ruin sex for ourselves if we are overly focused on an end goal. Sex and masturbation can be amazing and pleasurable even if they don't result in an orgasm. Instead of going into sex determined to reach orgasm, we should be going into sex determined to experience pleasure. If that ends with a climax, then great; if not, you haven't failed, as long as you had a good time.

Take me as I am

Good sex can never be experienced if the whole time we are on top we're worrying about whether our tits look saggy or our bellies are flopping. We often feel ashamed about how we look naked, especially if we experience changes to our body, for example post-mastectomy, or if we have scars or a disability, if we experience weight gain or loss, or a change to our shape after menopause. From our vulvas to our boobs, from our bellies to our bums, we are led to believe that they must all look a certain way in order to be sexually appealing to men and, as a result, we can end up thinking about them constantly during sex, especially if the lights are on. It is virtually impossible to reach orgasm if your mind is focused on how you look. Orgasms are as much psychological as they are physical. Even if you think you look great, being constantly focused on how he thinks you look will detract from your ability to truly enjoy sex. We spend so much time worrying about the size of our bums, or the tightness or wetness of our vaginas, or how it feels to him, that we forget to think about how it feels for us. The desire to impress men sexually – with how we look or feel – can ruin sex.

People might say that this isn't a problem that only women face. Men experience penis-shaming and anxiety about their size and appearance too. I am anti penis-shaming (unless they have shamed your vulva first) and I can grasp the impact on men who experience it; it must be incredibly anxiety-provoking. But, for women, it is compounded by the larger expectations for us to look sexy, which stem from how much society conflates women's sexuality with our worth and value. A man can turn up in a pair of raggedy boxers for first-time sex, while we are often expected to wear uncomfortable lingerie. I'm ashamed of the amount of time and money I have wasted on men who barely bothered to spray on a bit of aftershave before seeing me. I have endured painful waxes for men who haven't so much as trimmed their bush. I have spent hours in nail shops getting manicures and pedicures for men who turned up with smelly trainers and toenails that looked like they were last cut in 2018.

We have been led to believe that we have to be smooth and hair-free, that we have to paint our faces to look sexy and wear spangly underwear to get men hard, while we accept their sagging balls and spotty bums, we accept that their dicks smell like dicks, not like pineapples or roses, we accept their bellies and bald patches – we accept men completely as they are. We need to wake up and realize that most decent men accept us as we are too: it's only the misogynistic, narcissistic guys that are put off by reality.

The fact that completely normal and common things have come to be seen as flaws is so problematic. Mainstream porn has a lot to answer for, as do media portrayals of airbrushed, Photoshopped women. We have become so used to seeing completely distorted views of the female body that it has warped our idea of what is normal. We carry this from so early on in our lives, and it can completely fuck us up. Comparing ourselves to other women, especially other women who have had surgery or are under studio lighting or using clever camera angles, is damaging. We need to normalize normality: that includes spots from ingrown hairs, and cellulite on your belly, and folliculitis on your thighs, and stretchmarks on your pubis, and blackheads on your groin, and boobs that hang into your armpits when you lie down. It is all so fucking normal, and we need to accept every inch of our normal selves in order to have great sex. It's a cliché, I know, but the right man will not be put off by your body in any way, and if he is, then he's absolutely not worth fucking. You cannot be good in bed if you're not a grown-up. If he's expecting a flawless, hair-free, pert, teen-like body from an adult woman, then he has a whole load of scary issues that he needs to unpick in therapy and so a rejection from him is a very lucky escape.

I think it is important to mention herpes (HSV) here, as I get an abundance of messages from women who have been diagnosed and feel like their sex lives are over as a result. Two-thirds of the world's population have herpes simplex one (cold sores on the mouth) and one in six people has herpes simplex two (sores on the genitals, though it can also be transmitted orally). Eighty per cent of those people don't know they have it because they have never had an outbreak.

> **It is common, it is not dirty, and it does not mean that your sex life is over.**

Loads of children have the virus; it does not have to be sexually transmitted – you can get it from kissing your nan.

It is perfectly normal to see people with oral herpes (cold sores) without freaking out, but there is a stigma surrounding genital herpes that often makes women feel completely destroyed when they first have

the

right man

will not

be put off

by your body

in any way,

and if he is,

then he's

absolutely

not

worth

fucking

an outbreak. I say women because, according to Dr Naomi Sutton (@drnaomisutton, a sexual health specialist), there is a definite disparity across genders in their reaction to being diagnosed with an STI. Women tend to ask lots of questions, particularly about how to keep others safe; we cry, panic and worry that our lives are over and that no man will ever want us again. Whereas cis men tend to shrug and accept it. It is important to note that informing partners is the right thing to do in terms of keeping everyone safe. However, this can feel like a mammoth task because it comes with so much worry about being judged or rejected.

Given that the risk of contracting herpes can come from anyone you sleep with, whether they have been previously diagnosed or not, it means that anyone choosing to have sex with anyone runs the risk of becoming infected. So someone could reject you for disclosing your HSV status and then go on to contract it from the next person they sleep with. This is why education around herpes is so vital – if someone understands HSV, then they will understand that sleeping with you when you have consciously disclosed it and when you are committed to keeping them safe is no riskier than sleeping with anyone else in the wider population. When you choose to disclose, you should be armed with as much information as possible so that you can educate them about the facts, and if they choose to reject you after that, then it's purely based on their own ignorance and misunderstanding – and they are probably a bit of a dickhead anyway.

You can have sex safely with someone who has had a previous diagnosis of genital herpes in the same way that you can safely kiss people who have had cold sores. But the stigma is pervasive and, as a result, a diagnosis can be something that takes a long time to accept. When it comes to this specific thing, we need to be more like men and take an STI diagnosis in our stride: we need to accept that we are human and that illness and disease will probably happen to us all at some point, and that none of it makes us gross, even if it's sexually transmitted. HSV does not impact on your attractiveness, your worthiness or your ability to have great safe sex in the future. All of this also applies to HPV – listen to my podcast with Jo's Cervical Cancer Trust for more on this.

Love hurts; sex shouldn't

Phrases like 'giving yourself to him' or 'giving it up' are common and reinforce the notion that we are having sex for a man, not for us, and that we shouldn't really expect pleasure. We are taught that we are supposed to give our bodies up for men and allow them to fuck us any which way they like. Rough, repetitive thrusting in and out of the vagina with only a brief blow job for foreplay is the norm in mainstream porn. Men learn from this. Porn isn't all bad, but the vast majority of accessible free porn depicts very little female pleasure and very few real orgasms. Ninety per cent of my poll respondents said they had experienced pain during sex; 73 per cent said that they had tolerated painful sex and not said anything. It's tragically common among women who are subjected to the kind of sex that men have seen in porn. A lot of porn shows violence and degradation of women. Some men are emulating violent porn with women because they believe that that's what we want; other men do it because they enjoy hurting women and don't care about us at all. But sex isn't supposed to hurt, and if it does, then we must make it clear we want to stop. We have the right to withdraw our consent, but barriers can get in the way of us being able to do that easily.

Women have to know that they have the right to say no and to understand that if saying no puts a man off, then you have had a lucky escape. It can be hard to voice the fact that you aren't enjoying something, especially if you like the guy and you don't want him to think you're bad in bed.

But if he's hurting you, then he's the one who is bad in bed and he needs to know.

If you're worried that he will turn nasty, then you are with the wrong man. Being frightened of your partner's reaction when you say no to sex or certain sex acts means that you are in an abusive relationship, and you need professional support to address this. If you're worried that you'll seem frigid compared to other women who can 'take' rough sex, or that you'll be called a prude, then you need to own that. I don't know any men who aren't into masochism who would tolerate sex that was painful. Do you? If we accidentally knelt on their balls, they would say something, so why are we staying silent when their rough thrusting is hurting our cervix?

There are, of course, women who enjoy extremely rough sex, while others seek gentle and slow pleasure. But it's the painful sex that has been normalized. Men raised on memes and mainstream porn know little else. They believe dick-pounding repeatedly until the woman is in pain is exactly what every single woman they have sex with desires. I recently received this message from a man: 'I didn't know anything until I was in my mid-twenties. Too much porn made me think that women liked being talked down to and fucked hard and fast. I feel ashamed of the way I treated women in bed, but I really believed that that was what they liked.' Women accept this awful porn version of sex because they believe that the reason this rough sex doesn't feel good is because there must be something wrong with *them*. It seems to work for everyone else so they fake it to make it stop or because they are emulating porn, and the guy finishes believing he is *the man*.

Teenagers routinely believe that sex is supposed to hurt for girls. Girls are taught to expect pain when they lose their virginity. How sad is that? Why didn't anyone tell us that it shouldn't hurt? Why weren't we explicitly told that we should stop the second it felt painful? Why didn't anyone tell us that it wouldn't hurt if our partner made us wet, relaxed and comfortable, and that if he wasn't doing that, then he was getting it wrong? We have to have these conversations with our daughters and, perhaps even more importantly, with our sons. I will go more deeply into this in Chapter 8.

Communicate boldly

We should not be having sex with people who we can't communicate our true feelings to. It is common for us to feel shy, awkward, embarrassed or afraid of communicating our sexual needs and desires. The fragile male ego makes it doubly hard. Have you ever tried to have a conversation with a man where you explain that penetrative sex is not actually the holy grail and that over 70 per cent of women will need clitoral stimulation to cum? They don't like it. Every man I have said this to has responded with 'Every woman is different. You can't speak for all women.' Okay, then, if every woman is different, then why are you fucking us all the same way? Why aren't you asking at the start how we like it and whether we are a clit or a g-spot kinda gal? As women, we often stay quiet for fear of offending men, hurting their feelings or putting them off, often at the expense of our own pleasure. But we have to find a way to let them know what works for us and we must not be willing to sacrifice years of good sex because we don't know how to tell them how we like our clits rubbed. Do the work to let go of the shame that stops you from using your voice: shame that you carry about sex from religious, societal or cultural beliefs you've been brought up to accept. Let go of shame about your body and feeling undeserving of pleasure as a result. Let go of shame that you have internalized from misogynists about women and sex, shame from previous trauma, shame about health conditions and disabilities. We carry so much shame, and it can ruin things for us. We can't let go fully to experience pleasure because our subconscious is telling us that we shouldn't be doing it, or it's not feeling good but we just can't express it.

> **Sex is for us and we must feel empowered to say what we need from it.**

Set your boundaries. What is it that you will not accept or would never want to try? Be clear on that in your mind. Remember that boundaries can change; you may think you want to give something a try but then you change your mind back to it being one of your no-gos. That's okay. Your boundary can shift in a millisecond. You still have the right to assert yourself and not to engage with sexual acts that make you feel uncomfortable. Women have been conditioned to believe that we aren't able to put our feelings above a man's sexual needs. It can be especially hard if we feel that our boundaries might put someone off. It can be tempting to change your boundaries or to drop them completely in order to please those who don't respect them. Fuck. That. Shit.

Celibacy helps

Celibacy changed my life. From the age of fourteen, when I first started having sex, I never really had a period of being single. I was co-dependent and reliant on men for validation. I did not feel good about myself if I didn't have a man giving me attention. In 2016, I decided to make a conscious decision to be totally and completely single. I spoke to a few guys along the way, but I was very clear in my mind that I did not want to have sex. After a while, my relationship with myself changed significantly. I didn't want men to validate me, so I began to validate myself. It made me view sex completely differently. I felt horny at times, but that was easily resolved alone. I suddenly became more aware of how precious my body was. I remained celibate for eighteen months, and I haven't had bad sex since. It gave me a chance to reset and reclaim my body. It gave me a chance to love myself without any wobbles caused by men. It allowed me to understand my boundaries and to feel real ownership over my body. It was the best thing I ever did. Celibacy is one of the greatest tools in your anti-fuckboy toolkit, and it doesn't have to last a long time. Three months can be enough for the reset to happen.

The climax

We must not beat ourselves up for having bad or regrettable sex. We have no reason to be ashamed or embarrassed about anything that we have tolerated, or by how many people we have slept with. We are not alone. Bad sex is an epidemic that has existed for years. It is not us; it is them. We must not berate ourselves for the shit sex we have had before but instead commit to making sure that it's better in the future. Those of us with sons must teach them about the dangers of porn and the importance of pleasure and consent, and those of us with male friends should make sure that they are engaged in conversations about how sex with women needs to change. We will be unashamed, vocal and empowered, we will set our boundaries and own them like bosses. We will expect pleasure and we will teach our daughters to expect it too. We will change the narrative and close the gap.

We must not beat ourselves up for having bad or regrettable sex.

Chapter 8:

We can't consent to this

Last night I slept with a man I've been dating for a month. He is a nice, normal 40-year-old man who has shown no red flags or weird behaviour. He completely changed as soon as we were naked. He grabbed my throat and squeezed until I nearly blacked out. Then he took off the condom without warning – which I did not discover until I saw it on the floor mid-act. He was rough and the sex was painful. But I didn't say stop; I found myself moaning and acting as though I was having a good time. As soon as we finished, he was lovely again. He stroked my hair and we slept spooning. I left his house this morning and burst into tears. He treated me like a sex doll in bed. There was no pleasure, no communication, I was just there while he was doing whatever he wanted, and I allowed him. It didn't occur to me to tell him to stop, even though I was terrified and in pain. Why did he do this? Why did I respond like that? Should I give him a chance because he is lovely outside of the bedroom?

*U*nexpected, non-consensual rough sex is sadly an all too common occurrence for women. I hate how unsure of ourselves we can become in situations like the one described on the previous page. I hate the fact that we can feel concerned about sex acts that are being performed on us and still not use our voices. I hate the fact that if you had started punching a man and twisting his testicles without his consent, he would probably have stopped proceedings and blocked you immediately, no matter how sweet you were outside of the bedroom. I hate the fact that part of the reason he thinks this is acceptable is because many of the women he has slept with previously have probably pretended to enjoy it, confirming to him that *all* women love rough sex. I hate the fact that no matter how old you are, if you are a heterosexual woman on the dating scene, then there is a high likelihood that you will encounter men who think it is okay to fuck you like this without consent.

There are two answers as to why men do this – either he's a misogynist who gets off on hurting women in bed, or he has learned from violent porn that this is what women like and he has no idea that this is not okay. This is not an acceptable excuse. If he hadn't taken off the condom without consent, then there could be an argument for the latter, but condom removal without consent is rape (it's called 'stealthing' and there have been convictions against men in a number of countries for this, including the UK). That act alone confirms that he is a dangerous man with zero respect for you or regard for your safety.

As women, it can be hard to accept that it is not our fault when things like this happen. Victim blaming and shaming attitudes are rife across traditional and social media. We know that when women speak out about rape and abuse, the first questions people ask are often why we didn't say no, why we didn't scream, why we didn't call the police, why we stayed so long. I've even seen comments on nasty banter pages asking why we were even in bed with a man in the first place if we didn't want to be raped. It is hard not to internalize attitudes that have dominated the social discourse our entire lives – that men want and enjoy sex and that women are just vessels for their pleasure, and that if a man does something without our consent it's because *we* didn't gatekeep properly – 'boys will be boys', after all. It makes us question ourselves and what we did to cause the horrible things that happen to us, rather than being confident in the fact that no matter what we do or say, or where we go, or how we dress, we can never *cause* ourselves to be raped, assaulted or abused.

> **You cannot provoke abuse, you cannot ask for it, you cannot bring it on yourself.**

It is never, ever your fault. Even if you decide to go to a stranger's house after meeting him on Tinder, even if you got blind drunk on a date. Abuse is caused by abusers, and that is it. If someone performs violent sex acts on you, including anal, spitting, choking, slapping or hair pulling, without consent, then that is abuse.

The victim blaming and shaming we witness in cultural conversation can cause us to question what really is abuse or an assault. Social media, porn, movies and music have all normalized this idea that women should be okay with being hurt. Memes with images of a woman in pain along with statements like 'When he is bruising your cervix up, but your mum didn't raise a quitter' promote control and violence as being sexy and aspirational and lead people into normalizing dangerous relationships and harmful sex. The language used on social media to describe sex with women is shocking. You will often hear men talking about wanting to 'destroy' a pussy; some people even refer to sex as 'beating' or 'smashing'. Yet the same violent ideas about savaging vaginas don't seem to extend to penises. It would not be very well received by men if we went around saying things like 'I want to smash your dick up' or 'I'm going to beat your cock until you can't walk any more.' We have to recognize the misogyny behind all of this.

The normalization of this type of language means that we see it everywhere when men are talking about sex with women, and it makes us believe that in order to meet their sexual expectations we need to aspire to be a 'freak' who is willing to take anything in bed. We know we don't like it, we know that it hurts; mentally and physically, we know that if we saw someone else being treated in the way that we are being treated we would be clear that it was toxic behaviour, but when it comes to ourselves it can be harder to recognize abuse or assault, for a myriad of reasons. We don't believe that we deserve better, we don't know any different because we grew up in an abusive household, we believe that all relationships/sexual interactions are like this. We convince ourselves that it is normal and that a quiet, submissive woman is who we need to be to get the man.

It's tough out here. Dating as a woman comes with dangers. This shouldn't mean that we're terrified by all interactions with men, but the reality is that you need to consider safety in order to avoid scary dates and abusive partners. This chapter is not designed to scare you, it's designed to give you knowledge that will help to keep you safer. It will also help you to know that anything that has happened or might happen was absolutely not your fault, and you are not alone.

IF SOMEONE PERFORMS VIOLENT SEX ACTS ON YOU WITHOUT CONSENT, THEN THAT IS ABUSE

Dating dangers

Dating men can come with risks and, while we should not allow that to put us off meeting new people, it is essential that we keep it in mind. On more than one occasion, when I have told a guy that I'd like to have our first date in a public place for safety reasons, he's scoffed and said things like 'You think I'm going to rape you or something – lol – calm down, love.' But the fact is that it's very possible they might. Men who date women simply don't have to consider their personal safety in the same way when arranging dates, so they just don't get it – until they have daughters of their own.

A very close friend of mine went on a date with a man who seemed totally lovely. They had spoken for weeks beforehand and she was confident that she was safe in his hands. They met for dinner in a restaurant. She realized pretty quickly that he wasn't the man for her; she didn't fancy him in real life and their conversation was stilted. At the end of the date, she tried to part ways and get on the Tube to go home, but he insisted on accompanying her, saying that it wasn't safe for a woman to travel home alone. She tried to get rid of him, but he stayed with her anyway. As the journey progressed, he began talking about how depressed he was; he told her that he was unhappy and that life was getting him down. He went on and on with his tales of woe until they arrived at her front door. He asked if he could come in and call a cab. By this point, she was not feeling him at all and her gut instinct was going wild, but she felt guilty about making him wait in the street, especially because of how upset and depressed he was.

He came into her home, took his shoes off, lay down on her sofa and told her to get him a drink. She told him that she would rather he just called a cab. He instantly became aggressive and threatening and she demanded that he leave. He grabbed the tie of her wraparound dress and attempted to pull it off, so she screamed at him to stop. He then punched her in her face, fracturing her jaw and knocking her front tooth out. She begged him to go, but he refused to leave. He lay back down on the sofa and laughed at her while she called the police. They took over an hour to arrive, and when they did, she was hysterical, so they banished her to her own bedroom and forced her to stay in there while they asked the man what had happened. He made out that she was an escort and that she had attacked him.

The police believed him, despite her injuries, and no further action was taken.

We have both seen this man on dating apps since the incident and, despite reporting his page, he remains active on them. My friend is okay now, but it took a long time for her to heal both physically and mentally.

I did a story thread on IG where women shared their scary dating experiences and I received thousands of responses from women who had been raped and sexually assaulted on first and second dates. One woman wrote, 'I once went back to a Tinder date's house and he got upset when I tried to leave. I was left with bruises. I felt it was my fault for trusting him in the first place.' This sense of guilt and shame leads to women not reporting these incidents, so these men are free to return straight back to the apps to abuse other women. (I shouldn't need to say this, but the women who don't report are not to blame for this; the perpetrator is always to blame.)

Drink-spiking came up over and over again. One woman wrote, 'I met a guy who seemed great. After a lovely first date I agreed to go to his house for the second. I thought nothing of taking the drink that he offered me. I don't know what happened after that. All I know is that I woke up in hospital with all the physical signs that I had been raped. I have no idea to this day what happened.' Spiking happened both on first dates in bars and in men's homes. It is really worth watching Michaela Coel's *I May Destroy You* for an incredible depiction of spiking but also for a really nuanced look at all the issues around consent.

Stalking was mentioned by hundreds of respondents in my dating dangers thread. One woman wrote, 'A sweet guy walked me home after a first date. I wasn't up for a second meeting, but he seemed to take that well. That night as I was closing my curtains I noticed that he was still outside. Six months later I now have a non-molestation order against him because he ended up silently standing outside of my house for weeks and sending weird anonymous gifts to my home.' Erring on the side of caution, even with those men who seem harmless, is preferable to letting our guard down. I cannot emphasize enough how this is the one area where you shouldn't trust your gut – sometimes your gut is saying, 'He seems great, I'm sure it's fine to go to his house, despite the fact we've not met,' and even though your gut might be right, it's just not worth the risk.

Rough sex and choking

A recent study from the BBC shows that a third of women under the age of forty have experienced unwanted choking, hitting and spitting during sex[9], while NSPCC research shows that 40 per cent of teenage girls are experiencing coercion and violence during their first sexual experience.[10] And the saddest thing is that they are probably expecting it. They are seeing memes telling them that good sex includes violence and degradation and now many believe that this is how it's supposed to be. Let's not forget that this is also awful for boys too. For every girl who is pretending to enjoy it because it is now mainstream, there is likely to be a teenage boy doing the same. Boys are being robbed of the ability to enjoy gentle, pleasurable sex because they believe that they have to act like the

---

9   Harte, Alys. 'A man tried to choke me during sex without warning'. BBC News online, 28 November 2019. https://www.bbc.co.uk/news/uk-50546184

10 Kendrick, Keith. 'NSPCC Survey Finds 40 Per Cent of Teenage Girls Are Forced To Have Sex'. HuffPost, 11 February 2015 (updated 20 May 2015). https://www. huffingtonpost.co.uk/2015/02/11/nspcc-survey-finds-40-per-cent-of-teenage-girls-are-forced-to-have-sex_n_7316728.html

men they have seen hurting women in porn, or they see TikToks showing teen girls calling boys nerds for not being into sexual violence. It's all so warped.

One of the key questions that police and social workers ask victims of domestic abuse following an assault is whether there has been any history of choking or strangulation in the relationship. We ask this because nearly 50 per cent of women who were murdered by their partners or ex-partners had experienced strangulation by the man who murdered them within the year leading up to their death, making it a significant risk indicator for domestic violence homicide and attempted homicide. If a man has strangled you at any point within your relationship, there is a risk that he could go on to kill you. It is an act of dominance. When a man is choking you in bed, he is showing you that he has the power to kill you. Most of the men who claim that choking is sexy would baulk at the idea of being choked themselves; they understand very well that it is not an inherently pleasurable act; they would feel weak and powerless if a woman choked them and therefore do not see it as a standard part of sex when it is the other way around. We are apparently 'vanilla' if we don't want to be choked or hurt in bed – but, somehow, they have escaped that expectation and are only 'vanilla' if they don't wish to inflict those acts. It's much the same with anal, which of course some women love. But it has become another thing where there is this expectation that to meet the bar of 'freaky', we should be offering up our bum holes whether we like it or not. There is an assumption that women should just take it and enjoy it, but when we flip it around and suggest pegging them, they don't like it.

Choking is dangerous, whether done with consent or not. Consent has to be knowledgeable and informed to truly be consent, but how many people are considering, or are even aware of, the potential risks when they do consent to an inexperienced man with no formal BDSM (bondage, discipline, sadism, masochism – a niche sexual practice centred around consensual power and control in the bedroom) training choking them? According to research by the campaign group We Can't

Consent to This, in the UK alone twenty women a year are killed by being choked by a man during sex; in 1996, it was two women a year. It is no coincidence that this ties in with a rise in violent and more accessible porn, as well as the normalization of it by *Fifty Shades of Grey* and memes on social media. The more normalized and mainstream it becomes, the more women are dying. In that time, seven men have been killed as a result of choking during sex, and they were all killed by men. It is a potentially fatal act. Breath play (a dangerous act that should be practised with caution in which blood flow to the brain is constricted, causing light-headedness, then released to intensify orgasm) has now been banned in most fetish clubs because it is so dangerous. It takes seconds for a person to go into cardiac arrest when they're being strangled. The hyoid bone can be easily snapped, even with minimal pressure. Choking can result in life-changing injuries, including brain damage, heart attack, incontinence, blindness, bleeding and swelling inside the neck, risk of stroke and vocal-cord damage.

> **Did any of us really consent to risking those potential outcomes when we consented to being choked?**

Way too many of us have put ourselves in the line of fire, and it wasn't even for our own pleasure: we risked brain damage and permanent blindness because we wanted a guy to think we were good in bed. This has to stop.

I do not want this to be read in a way that suggests that I think any form of throat-holding during sex is a bad thing, because I don't. In fact, with prior expressed consent, I enjoy having my neck held very lightly by a man I wholeheartedly trust. I also don't want this to be taken in a way that suggests that I don't understand the appeal of erotic asphyxiation or breath play, but the current trend for choking being seen as a standard part of sex does not encompass either of those things, and the woman quoted at the start of the chapter highlights a common way in which this kind of act is done to women without consent or care. That guy was not thoughtfully practising breath play, he was harming her in a dangerous way. We've got to see it for what it is.

I have never been able to speak about the issues around rough sex without receiving backlash from people who believe that it is kink-shaming. It is really important to remember that there is no shame in enjoying rough sex in any form, but the 20-year-olds making videos on Snapchat about 'vanilla' sex being substandard and wanting to find a girl who they can strangle and spit at are not practising BDSM, they are co-opting the term in order to legitimize their desire to abuse women and girls. Consent is at the heart of the BDSM community: in order for it to be BDSM, not abuse, the four pillars of BDSM have to be at the heart of all sexual interactions. They are trust, communication, honesty and respect. If these are not in play, it is not BDSM. BDSM is about an exploration of power exchange and mutual pleasure; subs and doms have clear communication all the way through, everything is discussed in advance, safe words are pre-arranged and safety is paramount. It is not kink-shaming to say that choking practised without these four pillars is abusive.

On a recent Instagram post about the dangers of normalizing violent sex and the importance of consent, a man commented, 'It's up to a woman to say what she likes and doesn't like. We (men) can't mind read. If I'm in the middle of sex, I won't stop and ask, "Can I choke you?" I will be dominant and sexy and just do it. If she doesn't like it, she will just tell me to stop. Grow up, stooooopid.' Sadly, he speaks for many men. The assumption that all women want to be dominated is common, and it is scary. The assumption that it is sexy to choke, slap or hit during sex without warning or consent is even scarier. Asking for consent can be extremely sexy; it doesn't have to be mechanical and nor does it have to interrupt the flow. The man could say, 'Would you like it if I put my hand around your throat?' or 'Choking you would really turn me on right now, would that be a turn-on for you?' or he could initiate the conversation way before you even reach the bedroom. There are many ways to establish whether someone is comfortable with something you want to do to them.

A different man on the same post went on to say, 'If my penis is in her vagina, I'm pretty sure I have consent. All my sexual partners have enjoyed being choked.' But have they, or were they like the woman at the start of the chapter? Were they too shocked or scared to say no? Cis men tend to be physically bigger than cis women.

> **If you have a six-foot-three, fifteen-stone man on top of you with his hand around your throat, it really isn't that easy to say no.**

Sometimes we fear a scary reaction and we stay silent; sometimes we stay silent because we don't want to appear sexually inadequate or prudish; sometimes it's because we don't want to put him off; sometimes we feel like we are supposed to enjoy it because everyone else seems to and so we tolerate it because we believe that there must be something wrong with us for not liking it. And sometimes we believe, just like the arsehole in my comments, that because we have consented to sex, we have therefore consented to allowing the other person to do whatever they want. Consenting to one thing is not implied consent for anything else.

To be clear, absolutely loving violent sex is not shameful, and if you do, the above does not apply to you. It applies to the women who have tolerated it or pretended to like it because they felt they had to. It is for those women who felt ashamed because they didn't say no or couldn't say no. It is for the women who might find themselves with a hand around their neck and not know what to do next. We have total autonomy over our bodies, and we have the right to say no. If we find ourselves in a situation like the one described at the start of this chapter, we have to battle through all of the niggling doubts in our mind and assert ourselves and say, 'I do not like this. Stop.' If that means that he never wants to see you again, then you have had a lucky escape. If he doesn't stop, then that is rape.

WE HAVE TOTAL

AUTONOMY

OVER OUR BODIES

AND WE HAVE

THE RIGHT TO

SAY NO

Rape and sexual assault

This is the Metropolitan Police's definition of rape and sexual assault [bold words are my emphasis]:

> *Rape is when a person intentionally penetrates another's vagina, anus or mouth with a penis, without the other person's consent. Assault by penetration is when a person penetrates another person's vagina or anus with any part of the body other than a penis, or by using an object, without the person's consent.*

> *The overall definition of sexual or indecent assault is an act of physical,* ***psychological and emotional violation*** *in the form of a sexual act, inflicted on someone without their consent. It can involve forcing or* ***manipulating*** *someone to witness or participate in any sexual acts.*

> *Not all cases of sexual assault involve violence, cause physical injury or leave visible marks. Sexual assault can cause severe distress, emotional harm and injuries which can't be seen – all of which can take a long time to recover from.*

Rape and assault can occur in same-sex and gender non-conforming couples as well as heterosexual couples, but the terminology I am going to use here puts an emphasis on cis heterosexual couples. It is rape if you consented to penetration and then changed your mind but he didn't stop. It is rape if you agreed to do it because he made you feel worried or scared about saying no. It is rape if you are in an established relationship or marriage and he has sex with you when you did not want him to. It is rape if you consented to one type of sex, for example vaginal, but he put it in your anus. It is rape if he has sex with you while you are asleep. It is rape if he takes the condom off without your knowledge or consent. It is rape if he threatened to leave you for saying no and that's the only reason you agreed. It is rape if you agree to sleep with him to avoid being raped. It is sexual assault if he did any of the above without penetrating you with his penis. It doesn't matter if you were drunk, or high on drugs (and him being high or drunk is not an excuse – substances do not cause sexual violence or assault; abusers do). It doesn't matter if you were lying naked in his bed, it doesn't matter if you sent a hundred texts that day telling him how much you wanted to fuck. The minute that you no longer consent, or you are unable to, it becomes a criminal offence and an abusive act.

Sex acts obtained by deception are also non-consensual. Joyce Short, author of *Your Consent* and *Carnal Abuse by Deceit*, gave a TED talk in which she stated that for consent to truly be consent it has to be 'freely given, [a] knowledgeable and informed agreement'. If you agree on the face of it, then that is assent – but it's not consent if you weren't given the full facts. For example, if you are seeing someone and you think his name is Danny and he's a 31-year-old lawyer from Watford with no kids, but it turns out he's called Gary and he's a 19-year-old mechanic with six kids by seven women, then you were duped by an actor. You essentially had sex with a stranger; you did not consent to have sex with Gary. Your agency to make decisions based on the real facts was removed. It's a form of assault. It's the same if someone who absolutely knows that they only intend to have a one-night stand with you persuades you into bed with the promise of deep feelings and a long-term relationship, knowing full well that they are never going to see you again. If you had sex under these false pretences, then it is essentially assault (in the police definition above, assault includes emotional and psychological manipulation). As Joyce Short says in the same talk, 'They undermine your self-determination over your own body by deception.' Simply put, this means that you cannot give informed consent if you don't have all the facts. It's a cruel violation.

Some people might say that to call this assault demeans the experiences of people who have survived more violent assaults and rapes, and of course assault occurs on a spectrum. If you had your door kicked in by a maniac who robbed you at gunpoint you'd likely be severely traumatized, but you'd also be traumatized if you let someone into your home thinking they were a plumber but it turned out they were a burglar. Having your agency over your body removed is violating. Lads' banter and memes often praise and encourage the act of persuading people into bed, and we have to stop acting like this is normal. We need to see it for what it is. You might not get a criminal charge against someone who assaults you in this way, and nor would you probably want to, but you can still get justice in recognizing it for the evil act that it is, knowing it wasn't your fault, and from knowing that you're not 'stupid' and that you have nothing to be ashamed of.

Many of us will have been in the situation (particularly in our teenage years) where we feel that we have been led into sexual activity in a way that wasn't forceful or scary but where the pressure of the situation takes over and you have an almost out-of-body experience. You can see yourself doing things that you don't want to do, but you don't say no. You want to stop yourself, but the situation you are in feels hard to stop while you are in it. A good example of this is a scene from the documentary *Liberated* about sexual 'liberation' during American spring break, which you can find in my IG story highlights under 'Coerced Consent'. A young woman meets a guy who is very complimentary and says everything she wants to hear. She is then surrounded by his mates, who are loud and encouraging of the flirtation between the two of them. She says that she doesn't want to have sex with anyone because it is dangerous, which prompts him to quickly drop her and walk away. This combination of saying what she wants to hear and then rejecting her for not being up for sex is a powerful one, and within about ten minutes, the woman ends up going to his bedroom anyway. The sex lasts for about five minutes and the scene ends with her running away while the guy and his mates laugh at how easy it was to get her into bed and joke about the smell of her on his fingers. And even though she consented, I don't think she consented to the experience she had. I don't think she consented to her body being used quickly and thoughtlessly, or to being the butt of their jokes, or to being called easy. She consented in practice, but not in theory. The coercion she experienced was extremely subtle; the techniques he used were based on the knowledge that women are expected to perform niceness and politeness for men. They both shared the same sexual encounter, but they had very different experiences. He left feeling like a big man and she left feeling humiliated.

When I posted about this, too many women recognized this feeling and contacted me to say that they'd felt shame after a similar situation, sometimes even years later. This kind of coercive consent often happens on dates: you don't want to participate in sexual stuff, but you don't find yourself emphatically saying no. You go home afterwards replaying it all in your head, thinking, 'Why the fuck did I just do this when I really didn't want to?' If you are somebody who recognizes this, it might be worth reading up on the 'fawn' response to traumatic situations, as it gives some explanation of how we sometimes find ourselves in those out-of-body moments.

We need to ensure that the children in our lives are raised with very clear information about enthusiastic consent from as young an age as possible. Enthusiastic consent means a very clear 'yes'. We need our children to know that 'no' doesn't mean 'yes', or 'keep trying to persuade me', even if they are giggling while saying 'no' and they have a strong feeling that the 'no' does mean 'yes', that it's not consent unless they are emphatically saying 'yes'. We need them to know that saying 'Stop!' or 'No' is never a bad thing – it's never rude, and if it makes them appear frigid, then that is no bad thing. We can start drumming these messages in by ensuring that we obtain our children's consent before touching them: for example, if you're playing a tickling game and your child is saying 'Stop!' through their laughter, you absolutely have to stop and check with them before carrying on. We give weird messages about consent to our children when we do things like forcing them to give auntie a kiss when they've said they don't want to; we tell them it's rude to say no. While this type of scenario seems innocent, the message it gives them is damaging. It tells them that they have no bodily autonomy and that they have to comply to please adults and people in positions of power. Our children really need to know that the only time they should be saying 'yes' is when they are desiring physical pleasure and intimacy. They need to know that the only time they should ever even want to have sex is to share respectful, mutual pleasure. If they have to persuade their partner or they think that they're not totally up for it, then they need to be very clear that they become rapists if they continue to pursue sex.

Staying safe

There is no way to truly avoid running into men who might hurt us in bed or on dates, but there are some key indicators that might give us an idea, like the language that a man uses about women, the way he approaches initial conversations, the social media content he follows and shares, the type of porn he's into and his attitudes towards feminism. Before we ever grace a man with our presence on a date or in bed, we should be having conversations that enable us to judge his standpoint on these things.

This is the dark side of dating, and while it is never our fault if we do miss the red flags, or spot them and stay anyway, it is essential that we are armed with the knowledge that can help to keep us safe. We should head into any romantic interaction with a very clear knowledge of the potential risks so that we can better protect ourselves from them. If you are unfortunate enough to end up on a date with someone scary, or in bed with someone who becomes abusive, do not ever blame yourself.

It is hard to read these things without becoming utterly terrified but, statistically, most dates you go on will be with nice men who would not wish to harm you, so this chapter should not put you off dating, it should just remind you of the importance of being extra-cautious.

It is essential that we are armed with the knowledge that can help to keep us safe.

Following some of these basic safety rules can certainly help:

- Do not put too much personal information on your dating profile. Nobody needs to know your surname, where you work or that you live alone. Similarly, do not give away too much information before you get to know them. You can let them know that you work in a shop – they just don't need to know which one.

- If you communicate with them on social media, make sure that your location is not searchable – for example, turn the maps feature off on Snapchat. You should also be wary of things like letting them order you an Uber after a date, as they will then have access to your address.

- Google them before you meet. I have spoken to women who have established that the guy they were talking to has served time in prison for murder from a quick Google search.

- Always arrange the first few dates in public places.

- Do not let them pick you up or drop you to your door. You may find that you really don't want this person knowing where you live.

- Make sure that someone knows where you are going and who you are with. And subtly let your date know that you have sent his photo to your mate.

Trust your gut.
Even if
it's just a
niggling
doubt,
back out
the second
your gut
feels off.

- Arrange in advance for a friend or relative to call you midway through the first date with a fake emergency, in case you need a get-out clause.

- Make sure your phone is fully charged and that you have mobile data before you leave in case you need to call a taxi or make an emergency call. It is essential that you have the means to get home safely. Never go on a date where you will be reliant on their help to get home.

- If something does go wrong, make sure you report it to the dating app. I would also urge you to report it to the police (though I am aware there are many barriers to doing this and it's not always possible), even if it's just so that they have a record of them and their behaviour on file.

- Trust your gut. Even if it's just a niggling doubt, back out the second your gut feels off. But remember you should always take full precautions, even if your gut says he's safe.

Details for Rape Crisis and the Survivors Trust can be found at the back of this book.

Chapter 9:

Block, delete, move on

I have had my heart and trust broken so many times that I am now frightened of meeting anyone new. At the same time, I know that I would like to have a partner at some point in the future. How can I make sure that I don't get hurt again?

My job involves speaking to hundreds of women every week about the awful things that men have done to them, from the relatively minor to the extreme. I am well versed in just how painful things can get and how bad things can be. But if I ran a restaurant review service and I spent my working days hearing about restaurants that have poisoned people, it wouldn't make me refuse to ever go to a restaurant again. I would just choose the restaurants I entered more wisely, and I would stop eating and leave as soon as I found a hair in my soup. I am aware that there are a lot of bad restaurants, but I love eating out, so it's worth the risk.

I believe that we all deserve love, romance and intimacy, if we want it. To me it is an important part of the human experience. I believe that it's good to step away from dating when you are in a bad place, and I don't think we should chase love, but I also believe that it's good to remain open to the possibility of it at some point in the future. Many of us will have reached points in our lives where we think that we never want to go near another man again, and that is understandable, especially after abuse and trauma. There is really no requirement to be in a relationship, and being in a relationship is not superior to being single; however, completely shutting yourself off from the prospect of ever letting romantic love in because you are terrified of being hurt is life-limiting.

I have been in dark places and felt visceral pain after being hurt by men. I have felt like there was no way that I could pull through. Every second of every hour of every day was consumed by them, consumed by thoughts of rewinding time, by gut-wrenching agony that I believed would only dissipate if I had them back, by grief and regret and self-loathing. I've been convinced that I could never love anyone again because I fucked things up with my soulmate.

With hindsight, it is a major blessing that we broke up. They were less like soulmates and more like cellmates.

My point is that we *can* recover from heartbreak, pain and trauma. Some of us take longer than others, some of us need professional support to do it, but we are all strong enough to move on. We can go from loving someone deeply to having no feelings for them whatsoever. Hurt is really shit at the time, but it's not so shit that you should limit your future because of it. That gives way too much power to people who, over time, can and will become completely irrelevant to your life.

You can't guarantee that you won't be hurt again. You just have to know two things: the first is that if you are hurt again, you will overcome it, and the second is that now that you know all the red and pink flags, you are much more likely to be able to spot someone who may hurt you sooner and to take action before you get in too deep. You don't need to expect it to go wrong or to look out for flags. You just need to react correctly if and when they do appear. Don't be on the hunt for red and pink flags – look instead for green ones. Make sure he's a decent man.

Decent man

Decent man is the fuckboy antidote. He can be found everywhere and anywhere, but we sometimes miss him because his emotional intelligence and kindness seem foreign and we freak out when a nice man likes us. But after we've done the work to overcome that and are ready for stability, we can start to recognize this guy because he will be consistent.

He believes that women are equal to men and he lives by that.

Don't be on the
hunt for red
and pink flags
– look instead
for green ones.

You can see it in his interactions with all women, from the way he treats hospitality staff to the kind of porn he watches. He doesn't derail conversations about protecting women by saying, 'Not all men.' He pulls up his friends and others if he sees misogyny in action or women being treated poorly. He listens to you, talks to you and values your opinions. He is comfortable with being vulnerable and is willing to share his feelings with you. He encourages you to have a social life and is kind to your friends and family. He boosts your confidence and makes you feel good. He supports your dreams and ambitions. He treats you as an equal and shares responsibility for things like housework, contraception and childcare. He accepts that it shouldn't just fall on the woman to pump hormones into her body to prevent pregnancy. He pulls his weight at home, and the burden of keeping the house clean and looking after children doesn't automatically fall on you because you're a woman. He owns up to it when he is wrong and doesn't try to deflect accountability.

He values you and brings out the best in you.

He is affectionate without expecting sex. He shows empathy and compassion to others. He is honest about what he wants and never makes you question where you stand. He considers your needs in bed. He asks for consent before trying new things. He is kind and patient with children and animals. He is not freaked out by periods and he doesn't expect grown women to have pre-pubescent, hairless bodies. He is open-minded and non-judgemental. He is your friend.

I know that some people will be scoffing at this and thinking 'You are describing a unicorn!', which is sad, because what I have described is very basic. If we keep acting as if good men are unicorns, then we just feed into a narrative that being a piece-of-shit man is acceptable. Believing that good men are rare does us no favours because it makes us more likely to stay in relationships with bad ones under the false belief that there is nothing better out there. It means that we set the bar too low for acceptable behaviour from men and therefore we tolerate things that we shouldn't. It makes us normalize fuckboy behaviour. It means that when men do something like cheating or punching a hole in the wall, we cast it off as just being what men do. Being controlling, violent, unfaithful and disrespectfully promiscuous are not male traits. They are character flaws that disproportionate numbers of men seem to hold, because society enables them to get away with it and tells them that they are alpha males if they display those traits.

There are millions of decent men out there, but toxic masculinity often declares these men to be 'simps', 'pussies' or 'beta males'. They are seen as lesser men because they respect women, and when we're stuck in the 'pick me' stage we buy into it. We feel uncomfortable with nice, respectful men and chase after those who treat us poorly because we have been conditioned to believe that that is what we deserve and that's just how real men are.

The whole thing about women loving bad boys is head-bangingly irritating, because nobody actually loves being treated badly. But it's not wrong to say that many of us (often because of attachment issues) are drawn to the bad-boy type because we think we can change him. We thrive on the chaos and uncertainty he brings, as it feels familiar and often there is something seductive about having someone who is hard and rough on the outside becoming vulnerable and soft in your arms. We are taught that being a real man means having no emotions, showing no weakness and fighting your way through life to be the toughest, most macho guy on the block while shagging as many women as possible. But these guys are in fact weak.

> **The guys who believe that they are alphas are nearly always narcissists with very fragile egos.**

They take the piss out of decent men for being simps when the truth is the opposite. Do you know how strong you have to be as a man to go against the grain? Decent men are by far superior. So it's worth holding out until one of them appears, and if that takes years, then so be it; it's better to be single for ten years than to spend ten months with a wrong'un. Keep the faith in good men – it will help to protect you from the bad ones.

When you do find someone and they appear to be waving green flags, you need to try to enjoy it. Enjoy them, enjoy the ride, enjoy it while it's good. It might last for ever, it might last for a summer – it doesn't really matter; what matters is that you had a great time with a new human. Just because he's a decent man doesn't mean it's always going to work out. Neither does it mean that you should force yourself to have a relationship with him. He can fit the bill of decent guy but still not be the man for you. Don't feel like you are obliged to give your time to people who you aren't into just because they are interested in you and they're a nice person. Being interested and being kind should come as standard: it shouldn't be seen as so rare that when you find one, you have to hang on to them.

> **An interested, decent man who makes us feel the feels is what we need to hold out for.**

They can be the nicest person in the world, but if we don't have chemistry or a connection with them, then they are not the person for us. It's better to be single than to settle with any old Tom, Dipesh or Gary simply because they are keen. You do not have to sacrifice your own relationship needs and desires just because a decent man is into you. Let them down gently, though, be kind and protect their heart, but don't get into something just because you don't believe you will ever find anyone better. Hold out for an all-rounder, someone who is interested and interesting.

If you find someone who seems to be that all-rounder, it's important to remember that even if things do go sour, you had fun while it lasted. Every time they made you feel wonderful was still real. Even if they turned out to be the world's biggest liar, and the decent-man thing was a masquerade, none of it was a waste of time. You got something positive out of it at the beginning. You had some excitement. There is no such thing as wasting the best version of ourselves or wasting our time on someone; it is all part of your life story. You don't just get one shot at being great before you expire; you're not a banana. You are an ever-evolving human whose best version of themselves changes and upgrades each time you are taught a lesson by someone who hurts you. If you showed the best version of yourself to a person who turned out to be a fuckbucket, then you can stand proud knowing that you tried – you made an effort, you showed up as your best self and you did what you needed to do to make things work. If that was unappreciated by the recipient of your desires, or it just didn't work out, then it wasn't a waste; it was simply a learning curve. It was only a waste if you didn't learn anything from it and if you jump into the next dating experience and overlook the same red flags that were waved at you during the last one. And if you do find yourself doing that, therapy would really help.

All cried out

There are few things worse than a broken heart. When I split up with my son's dad I listened to Alicia Keys' 'Try Sleeping with a Broken Heart' and Phil Collins's 'Groovy Kind of Love' on rotation. I was pregnant and I was on the floor, literally and metaphorically. I could not see a way out of the pain. I wailed for days, then sobbed intermittently for months. I was consumed with sadness, hate, rage, fear and self-loathing. I didn't even want him back; I despised him. Even after the very emotional period passed, I harboured hatred towards him for years. I started dating again when my son was about eighteen months, but I was still very broken after the split with his dad and I was dating because I wanted a man to heal me, to show me that I was worthy. I wanted someone else to take away the pain he had caused, so I was bringing this kind of desperate 'please love me and please don't hurt me' vibe to every date. My broken heart didn't heal until the day I forgave him. One day it just hit me and I mentally said goodbye to it all. I stopped needing closure, I stopped wanting an apology, I stopped replaying it all in my head, I stopped listening to Phil Collins. I

YOU DON'T JUST
GET ONE SHOT
AT BEING GREAT
BEFORE YOU EXPIRE.
YOU'RE NOT
A BANANA.

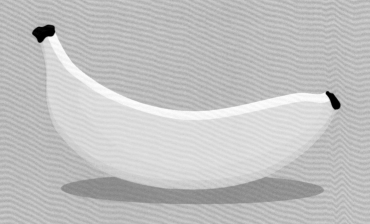

just decided I'd had enough. I said out loud, 'I forgive you. It's done.' And that was it – I shut the lid. Apart from the respect I have for him as a good father, I have no feelings whatsoever for him now.

My advice for bossing a break-up is to allow yourself to feel it all. Succumb to the pain; be fucking dramatic; cry; listen to extra-sad tunes that make you cry even more; pretend you're in an epic music video; ask your friends to listen to you; talk about it; wallow in it. Grieve. It is a form of bereavement. The future you had pictured is over, and even though the new future is going to be even better, it is normal to feel sad for the one you lost. But put a time limit on it. Get it all out and move forward. If you are still in a state of absolute despair and it's impacting on your daily life after eight weeks, then, please, get on the phone to a counsellor and book an appointment. I'm not saying that you will be miraculously healed at the eight-week mark, but there has to come a point when you take your power back and, sometimes, we need professional help to do that if we're not managing by ourselves. Of course, all of this becomes much more complicated if divorce or children are involved. If you can't access therapy, there are lots of self-help books and resources online. Abraham Hicks on YouTube works for me. Like magic, in fact. It's a bit like Marmite. Some people can't get over the fact that a woman called Esther speaks about herself in the third person on behalf of a ghost called Abraham. If I'm honest, I doubt I'd have even listened to it if I had known that back story. But I went into it with an open mind and just listened to what she had to say, and it has changed my life. There are thousands of videos on YouTube; you can search whatever it is that you need help with, for example 'Abraham Hicks pain after break-up' or 'Abraham Hicks single and lonely', and there will be something that you can apply to your situation. Flick through a few until you settle on one that resonates with you. (They won't be for everyone, though. My cynical, dry-witted mother would call me an absolute clown for recommending these, but if you're five weeks deep in a heartbreak hole, then what have you got to lose? The Law of Attraction has its flaws, but it just makes me feel better, reassured and more positive. It might work for you. Check out @megan_rose_lane on Instagram for more on this too.)

Writing a list of all the negatives about the person you have split up with can also help. Write down every single thing that you won't miss about them, from the irritating way they said the word 'almond' to the way they chewed, to the ways in which they hurt or disrespected you. Keep going back to this list every time you miss them. But keep reminding yourself that you are going to miss them intermittently in the future. You are going to have moments when something happens and your first thought is to text them to tell them about it. Or when you're finishing a night with your mates and they're all going back to their partners and you're going home alone. You will miss them, and you will want them, but you will also allow those moments to pass.

It can feel like recovering from an addiction. It's a battle, because while you hate the thing that you're addicted to for how it's impacting on your health and your life and you know it's bad for you, you still have strong attachments to it. It's been your way of coping and you can't imagine life without it. Withdrawing and recovering from a person is not dissimilar to recovering from an addiction. You have to go cold turkey if you really want it to be over. If you have children with that person, it makes zero contact impossible, but there are ways of managing contact to ensure that you have minimal opportunity to get sucked in by them. If necessary, you could ask someone else to facilitate handovers, like a neighbour or a friend. Or you can search for co-parenting apps like Cozi or Co-parently that help you manage your co-parenting schedule without any need for contact. But even if you do have to see them, it is still possible to diminish your emotional attachment to them over time.

The end of a short-term situationship can sometimes feel more traumatic than the end of something big. It feels embarrassing to grieve it because it was so brief and you feel like a dickhead crying to your friends about someone you only had two proper dates with. It feels like you should just be able to get over it. But some things just hit hard. Especially when the same pattern keeps repeating.

Many women on dating apps are experiencing the same cycle: winding up infatuated with men who are secretly no-labels fuckboys, frequently being ghosted or breadcrumbed, never getting past the third date, always being put in the sex-only zone or the friend zone, never being chosen as a girlfriend, experiencing constant rejection. When the same stuff keeps happening over and over again, it's hard not to feel crushed. It's hard not to internalize it as confirmation that you're not good enough. It feels like you are the common denominator. We convince ourselves that men keep treating us in this way because we aren't worthy of anything else. Then we continue on without having a period of reflection to work on how we feel about ourselves. Instead, we cling to people who have already made us feel like shit or get into things with new people who are inevitably going to do the same thing. Investing in people who have already treated you with ambivalence and indifference, waiting for them to change their minds and finally validate you by showing some interest – however limited – is quite literally soul-destroying.

Learn when to walk away. So much of this boils down to how you feel about yourself. It is much easier to walk away from things that are causing you pain when you know deep down that you deserve better, when you are certain that this person is not going to be your final option because you are clear that you have value and that the treatment you are receiving is because the other person is a prick, not you. You did not bring mistreatment on yourself, you just stayed around and tolerated it for longer than you should have, for all the reasons we've covered in this book.

We should absolutely strive to work through relationship problems that occur within healthy partnerships. All good relationships come with ups and downs, but we must not apply the same mentality to situations where we are predominantly unhappy and predominantly being taken the piss out of. It's like when you're at an after party and you start feeling tired and the vibe gets a bit shit and every bone in your body is telling you to go home, but you don't, because you're worried that you might miss out on some fun. Then you end up throwing up on a cream carpet and having to pay £200 for a carpet clean while wishing you had just listened to your gut and gone home five hours ago. Know when to leave the party. There will be more parties: don't stay at the shit ones just because you're worried that you'll never be invited to a better one.

This is, of course, much harder to do if it's abuse that you need to walk away from. You may need professional support to help you to leave, especially if there is a risk of violence. Leaving without a safety plan in place can be risky. Evidence shows that leaving a violent relationship is one of the highest-risk times. So, reach out to Women's Aid or Southall Black Sisters or Muslim Women's Network (more details for support services can be found at the back of this book), or google a domestic abuse support service in your local area and get help to start you on your journey to leaving. For Black women, this can be doubly hard. Kelechi Okafor notes that

> Black women are expected to love and uphold Black men no matter what they do. It's an age-old conflict: we want to protect ourselves, but protecting Black men is often the first instinct, because you know the violence that will be inflicted upon them by calling the police or informing authorities and handing them over to the state. This can keep Black women in abusive relationships for longer. Especially because social media (Clubhouse and Black Twitter) shuts down conversations about Black male perpetrators because they don't want Black men to be publicly put down. People protected Bill Cosby and R Kelly out of a misplaced sense of loyalty. Black Women see this and feel the barriers of speaking out. We are meant to be protected and valued by our men and if they don't protect us it's seen as our fault. I caused my bad treatment. It must be something I am doing wrong.

For Muslim women, leaving an abusive relationship is also incredibly difficult, because of societal and religious barriers, explains Munira from @muslimsexeducation.

Women can be spiritually guilted into staying by being told that the abuse they are suffering is religiously justified and that breaking up a family by leaving is sinful. There is also a narrative that obedience and submission to your husband is required, regardless of whether that is causing you harm, so from the religious perspective some women can be led to believe that there is no way out. There is also a stigma with being divorced and a level of shame that it can bring the woman's family. Pressure is often put on women to remain in abusive marriages, because it's better to be married than to be a divorced single mother. Conversely, due to societal views about Muslim women and the false perception that we are always downtrodden in relationships, and that Islam enables this, we are acutely aware of how us leaving can be used to justify Islamophobia. Muslim women know that abuse is not divinely sanctioned, but it's difficult to seek support as a Muslim woman when you know that your situation might be used to further propagate Islamophobic tropes.

It is really fucking hard to escape an abusive relationship. There are barriers for everyone who needs to escape. It is never easy, but it is always worth it. You are not alone and there is support available. Please seek it out. **They will not change.**

If it's not domestic violence that you need to run from, if it's just a relationship or situationship that's doing you more harm than good, then just pull the plaster off and go. You've got this.

Closure

When a relationship ends, we often tell ourselves that we need closure before we can truly walk away, but closure comes from within. You do not have to leave your house or even speak to another person to gain closure. Closure is a concept that we learned from romantic films; it is an excuse to go and see your ex one last time (or maybe twenty-five last times). You do not need it to be able to move on. We tell ourselves that we need closure when we are not really ready to let go. If you were ready to let go, you would gain closure for yourself by accepting that it's over and that you do not need to hear an apology, or an excuse; you don't need the dramatic goodbye or to go out with one final bang. Visiting someone for closure usually comes from there being a glimmer of hope that something might change. That's why seeking it often ends up with us feeling worse, because we end up sleeping with them, or we end up arguing, or they don't end up saying what we want to hear.

You could wait a lifetime to hear them admit to cheating, or to be given an explanation for why they ghosted, but does getting this really make any difference? An admission of guilt or a rationale being provided for why they hurt you doesn't change anything, it just eases their conscience. Especially because half the time their explanations are a load of bullshit, and the rest of the time they turn the issues back on you.

Don't pretend that you need closure in order to justify shagging your ex, or in order to not look like a dick when you tell your friends that you are meeting them one last time. Just go forth and own it – we've all had moments of weakness – but just make sure that you aren't harming your own progress as a result. You can get closure all by yourself.

Block, delete, move on

We can take back our power by blocking, deleting and moving on.

Blocking is not petty, and it does not have to be spiteful. It is symbolic, an act of protecting your space. It means you can't obsess over whether they will text you or like your pictures and it means you can't watch their social media or WhatsApp activity either. But in addition, you need to block them mentally. Mindfulness is extremely helpful for this. Mindfulness is a form of meditation that teaches you to focus on the present, so that when your mind wanders to thoughts of them, you have the tools to be able to bring it back to where you want your attention to be. When you become obsessed by thoughts of them, practise mindfulness and take control.

Deleting is important. Delete all traces of their number (unless you have kids with them, of course) and all old conversations. It means that you won't torture yourself by reading over it and wondering what went wrong. Having their phone number easily accessible in your phone makes it more likely that you might contact them during a moment of weakness, especially if you are drunk or feeling lonely. Having their conversation thread sitting in your WhatsApp means that you will occasionally see their profile picture when you are mindlessly scrolling through your chat list and that can send you back to square one and make you feel tempted to contact them.

Moving on is the key. Once you have blocked and deleted them, you need to work on self-love, self-care and learning from the lessons that this relationship has taught you. You *will* get over them; whether it takes weeks or months, you *will* eventually get to the stage where you wake up and you are not thinking about them and you will realize that it's over. Moving on doesn't have to involve another person. You don't have to move on to another relationship, you just have to move on mentally from the emotional ties to the last one.

My job involves hearing daily horror stories about men, but it also involves receiving daily messages from women who have found a partner who makes them happy or who have embraced being single and are having the time of their lives. If you are dating, you are definitely going to come across some fuckboys – it's inevitable – but the second you identify them for what they are, you should run like the wind.

> **Self-love is at the heart of making good decisions about men and it is essential that we strive for it.**

For me, it feels like a daily battle. I fluctuate frequently; sometimes I think I am an amazing catch and other times I feel like a disgusting hag. Simply saying 'You should love yourself' is meaningless, especially if you have been in abusive relationships (with your parents or a partner, etc.) and you have been made to feel worthless. Self-love takes action. For me, it's proper self-care, sticking to my daily skincare routine, going to the gym, eating well, drinking water, meditating, listening to Abraham Hicks, seeing friends. I have to force myself to love myself but, once I'm there, everything fits into place. We need to give ourselves the love that we so recklessly give to other people.

Honour your inner child

Think back to your three-year-old self. You are still her. The same beautiful little egocentric soul that came into this world loving the crap out of herself, you are her; she lives on inside of you. My three-year-old self would have been horrified if she could have had a look into her future. She would have really wondered why she was chasing after criminals with neck tattoos and getting ghosted by wastemen on Tinder. I have let her down many times, but I have learned that it helps me to look back to my early years to remind myself of my value. If a three-year-old girl walked in now and sat on your lap, you would see her with the world at her feet. You would know that she can be whoever she wants to be; you would see her and her future as precious.

> **You are still that girl, and it's never too late to honour her.**

Grab a photo of yourself as a child and tell that child that it's going to be okay. Tell her you're going to make her proud. And then think of her when the next fuckboy you encounter makes you feel bad – remember that she deserves better.

Remember you are a spectacular buff ting

A spectacular buff ting is a person who is buff to their core. It doesn't matter what they look like on the outside, they glow by virtue of the fact that, deep inside, they are kind and empathetic. A spectacular buff ting doesn't judge others because they have probably 'sinned' before and are pretty likely to 'sin' again in the future, several times over. A spectacular buff ting is someone who can acknowledge that they have behaved like a dick in the past and who does their best not to carry that behaviour into the future. It is someone who recognizes their flaws but celebrates their strengths. A spectacular buff ting knows that they are not defined by their past, and nor will they ever be made to feel ashamed of their choices. They do not feel the need to apologize for or to take the blame for past toxic relationships, and they do not apologize for taking up space or being vocal about their needs or opinions. A spectacular buff ting lifts other people up and helps others to learn from their mistakes. They try their best to take a balanced and calm approach to dealing with nasty or annoying people and they never resort to violence or spite. A spectacular buff ting knows themselves and what they deserve, they have high standards and they expect respect. They recognize red flags and they heed them. They treat other humans, and animals, with love and compassion. And on the days when they fuck up, they take ownership and they repair it. A spectacular buff ting lets go of society's expectations about how we should look and tries their best to show unconditional love to themselves. A spectacular buff ting does not always feel like a spectacular buff ting, and that's okay – we all wobble – we've just got to try to remember who the fuck we are. You were born a spectacular buff ting; we all were. We go off track sometimes because of trauma and life and all that shit, but we never lose it; it is in our souls. Harnessing your spectacular buff ting energy is one of the most powerful tools in your anti-fuckboy toolkit.

Every day is a fresh day, a new start, an opportunity to do better and make better decisions

Don't beat yourself up over what happened yesterday. Instead, take control of today and tomorrow. Live your best life: eat well, drink loads

Expect better,

remember your value

and who you are,

then elevate higher.

of water, move your body, be grateful, don't overthink, don't live with regrets, turn up your favourite music and dance, ring your friends and tell them you love them, post hot pictures of yourself for yourself, read books, go out into the fresh air, take walks, talk to animals, be unashamedly you and live every day with passion. Don't be afraid of getting hurt. Throw yourself into finding love, if that is what you want, but get yourself into a really strong single place first, so that if you do encounter a fuckboy, it won't ruin your entire life. Get to a place where you know the red flags and you are able to heed them, and where you see every failed encounter as a good story to tell your friends. Be free, be confident, have fun, and if you didn't manage that today, then there's always tomorrow.

Be unashamedly you and live every day with passion.

> 'You were born of the stars, dear girl. Stop settling for the dust they leave behind.' @daniel.peter.walsh

Expect better, remember your value and who you are, then elevate higher and reach for the stars to find your equal. And while you're on your journey, embrace the adventure . . . and **Block, Delete, Move On** from anyone or anything that disturbs your peace.

Charities to get behind

If readers are looking to offer more support to small grassroots organizations, please consider donating to any one or all of these groups. They work tirelessly to protect women and children while amplifying our voices, and they urgently need our support. I have chosen these five to support because they have all touched my life in some way and I aim to give a proportion of the book's profits to them. They have supported people I know, or I have worked with them professionally, and I have seen first-hand the impact that they have on people's lives.

Free Your Mind CIC

Free Your Mind CIC is a peer-led, not-for-profit children's domestic violence and trauma support service. It is the only service in the UK that focuses specifically on supporting children and young people who have witnessed domestic abuse in the home. It is entirely dependent on donations for its revenue stream. Your donations will go towards the provision of short- and long-term counselling and therapy for children and a safe space for them to receive advice and support, will help staff to run the web chat service for children and to provide advocacy and personal care items for them and their families. Your contribution will also help to fund their work in lobbying Parliament for changes to laws to further protect children and families in cases of domestic violence.

www.crowdfunder.co.uk/hear-my-voice-free-your-mind-cic

Southall Black Sisters

Southall Black Sisters is a leading organization for Black and minority women and girls in the UK. It is committed to the principles of equality and justice for all, but especially supports abused Black and minority women, one of the most marginalized groups in our society. It strives to provide a safe environment for women trapped in abusive relationships or at risk of violence and abuse.

Southall Black Sisters saved my friend's life after she fled from abuse. She was restricted by the fact that she was a non-UK citizen and so had limited rights. Without Southall Black Sisters, I don't know how she would have coped. They welcome donations to help them support all women, but migrant women in particular, who are subject to gender-based violence and immigration restrictions such as No Recourse to Public Funds (NRPF). Your donations will help them provide much-needed emergency accommodation, food and other subsistence support. For more information about their work and how you can donate and make a difference, visit their website at southallblacksisters.org.uk

Rights of Women

Every day, women contact the Rights of Women helplines because they are unclear or confused about how the law can help them. These women want to know their rights in all kinds of situations, for example if they have been assaulted by their partner, or raped, have fled their country because of violence, fear their children will be taken from them, have an insecure immigration status, have separated from their husband or have experienced workplace harassment.

The lawyers and staff at Rights of Women believe that all women have the right to accurate and accessible advice and information about the law and their legal rights. They believe that women need this advice and information to enable them to make safe and informed choices for themselves and their families. The law is complex and confusing. Rights of Women make sure that, at some of the most difficult times in their lives, women are able to talk to a lawyer who can give them expert and non-judgemental legal advice and accessible information about the law and their legal rights. Without this advice and information, women will continue to experience violence, abuse and discrimination and be unable to play an equal role in society. Your donations will help Rights of Women to deliver a range of high-quality and accessible services aimed at increasing women's understanding of the law and their ability to seek justice.

rightsofwomen.org.uk/get-involved/support-us/

We Can't Consent to This

We Can't Consent to This was started by an amazing woman called Fiona Mackenzie. She was shocked when she read a news story about a woman who was murdered by her partner in a brutal and sadistic manner. He received a light sentence because his defence was that it was a sex game gone wrong and that his victim had consented to 'rough sex'. Nobody consents to being murdered; sex should not kill. Fiona single-handedly collated information about murders in which the 'rough sex defence' was used to justify murdering women and realized that something needed to change urgently. A number of women joined forces with Fiona and together they formed We Can't Consent to This. All are volunteers and work tirelessly around their day jobs to lobby the government to end the use of the 'rough sex defence'. Their fight against the normalization of violence against women – particularly in relation to non-consensual choking – is some of the most vital work in the fight for gender equality happening at the moment. They need funding in order to keep on fighting this fight on behalf of all women, and on behalf of our daughters. Follow them at @wecantconsentto

The Triple Cripples

The Triple Cripples is a platform founded by Kym Oliver and Jumoke Abdullahi to address the lacuna in the media landscape when it comes to the visibility and narratives of those hidden from view and to bring the stories of disabled Black women, femmes and non-binary people into the light. There was literally no representation for these two women and so they decided to do what Black women have done historically when faced with inhumane and seemingly insurmountable challenges – they decided to be the change they wished to see and built their own platform.

The Living Archive is Kym and Jumoke's history-making, multimedia anthology of snapshots, videos, transcripts and audio from real-life conversations and interviews with disabled Black women, femmes and non-binary people from around the globe. This project will inscribe the presence of disabled Black folks into history in a way that has never been done before. It's a collection of personal stories from disabled femmes from all walks of life, every socio-economic status, profession, culture, sexuality, religion and nationality, interwoven with reflections from Kym and Jumoke. It tackles hard topics not discussed in 'respectable' society, discussing taboos, our cultures, our loves, our joys and defying stigma. The Living Archive attempts to address not only the lack of representation but the active erasure of disabled women, femmes and non-binary people of colour. The Living Archive will uplift and amplify the lives and voices of those that are here. It is imperative that we record their stories and highlight their narratives on a global scale.

Donate to this brilliant project at www.paypal.me/thetriplecripples or contact them at www.thetriplecripples.uk

Acknowledgements

This book would never have happened without the following people. I owe everything to all of you.

My mum, who enabled me to take the leap to change my career and who taught me everything I know about loving other humans and how to be an activist for those who need it. My son, who makes me proud every single day and gives me hope for the future of men. My sister, who hyped me all the way along and talked sense into me when I was having doubts: the best therapist ever. And my brother-in-law and nephew, you keep me and my boy going. Dad – you're going to hate this, put it down now. Nanny, the legacy of strong women started with you; E&H are continuing it along with me. R, I, V, B – this one's for Mumo. NB and GW, my honorary uncles, the best of men.

Grace, my left hand, my right tit, my carer, my probation officer, my PA, my social worker, my best friend, the biggest thank you. D, S, J, P, my community, my gang, my team, my best friends. This is for your daughters. G, this is also for my guide daughter. Lou, my whirlygig. E, szeretet. Jac G – my gooner. Laura A, it was meant to be.

My new family, Ivan Mulcahy and Jasmine McKell (and Rachel, who had to suffer Ivan spending hours with me on the proposal). Jasmine, you kickstarted it all; I am forever in your debt. Ivan, *the best* literary agent in the entire universe. You make me feel safe, supported and heard. You pushed me to make this happen. Tilly and all at IMB Creative. Helena Gonda, I absolutely love you. Becky Short and Sophie Bruce, what a team, so grateful that I got you. Everyone at Transworld, I am honoured to have been published by you. Thanks go to Cat Lobo (@thecatlobo) for designing the brilliant logo. Emma Jones, you gave me my first proper writing opportunity and I have loved working with you, Kelby and all the gang at *OK!* Cherry Healey, you were the first proper 'known' person to take me seriously; inviting me on to your BBC show was a huge kickstart to my career, you helped me endlessly. Chimmy Lawson, the Pinker Print, you were the catalyst.

The contributors to this book are all people who I highly respect in their fields and who I recommend that you follow. I want to give a huge thanks to the following people for their time and energy. I appreciate you all hugely.

Dr Mayowa Aina – clinical psychologist working for the brilliant charity Black Minds Matter UK: @dr.mayus

Dr Karen Gurney – clinical psychologist/psychosexologist and author of *Mind the Gap*. Karen read over the sex bits and guided me to make sure I was correct. Karen has taught me so much and I appreciate her work hugely: @thesexdoctor

Munira – Munira started out as a supporter of my page but has become a friend. I have learned endless amounts from her about the experiences of Muslim women when dating. I love you, Munira! @muslimsexeducation

Kelechi Okafor – actor, pole-dance-studio owner, public speaker, writer and general icon. Kelechi is an important voice on Instagram and Twitter: @kelechnekoff

Jo Westwood – co-dependency coach. Jo does invaluable work to help people to address and recover from co-dependency issues. She helped me massively with getting Chapter 3 right: @jowestwood

To the incredible people who read this and helped me to make sure that I was getting it right – Anny Ma, Sasha Mind Your Own Plants (and her friend Jeffery), the wonderful Emily Rose and Rose Ellis, Janah Jackman, Kym Oliver, Mike Hailu, Shona Landon and Njilan Morris-Jarra – thank you immensely.

Last, but absolutely not least, the following are all people who have given me faith in humanity. Brilliant, kind, compassionate people who have supported me like family, despite being complete strangers when they first found my page. They have not only enabled and supported me to continue fighting for a better dating landscape for women, they have enabled me to write this book. I love every single one of them, the biggest spectacular buff tings in the land, my patrons and Instagram supporters:

@abbie.does.dating
@babytoddlerfoods
@honestly.im.ok
@thirtysomethingsingle
Abigail Ryan
Aileen Barratt
Aimie Smith
Alisha Thimble and Doll
Amy Cally
Amy Parsons
Anna
Anna Fay
Anna Patricia
Anna Sinfield
Annika
Arreebeeeeseeseeayyyyy
Barbara Keller
Beanie Bea
Becca Campbell
Becks Brown

Ben Hyde
Beverley Tipping
Briony Crump
Bryony
Caitlin Heal
Caroline Brady
Cathy @thatsinglemum
Cez Thomas
Chelberto
Charlie Sydenham-Brackstone
Chrissy
Christina
Claudia Kühler
Cleo
Danielle Murphy
Deejronimo
Delightful Dan
Desmond and Pauline (Shay)
Donna and Alice Smith
E.claire.good

Ebony Staite Dagnall
Elaine Downie
Elferg Yolanda
Emma Bronson
Emma Fairclough
Emma Green
Emma Lardner
Emma Linfield
Emma Louise Daly
Emma Wilkinson
Empress Success
Emzy Lou
Esther S
Eunika Adams
Fareeda Butt
Felicity Loud
Frilly
Gabriele
Geemarmite
Gemma Harrison
Gina
Hannah Ocee
Harriet Stokes
Hattie Delves
Hayley Tanks Mommy
Helena Brackee
Holl Wanderlust
Holly Ems
Hope Stubbings
Ijys
Iola
Isabelle Jackson
It's me, Ayşe
Iyecha Corblimey

Jack Linzell
Jade Lianna Woods
Jade Neilson
Jade Subaney
Jaz Fleur
Jemma Sheridan
Jen Can You Fucking Not Hun
Jengles
Jennifer Britton
Jo Parkinson
Joanne McLaughlin
Jordan B
Joy's World the Podcast
Kate
Kate Chivers
Katie McLean
Katy Whitelock
Kaumal
Keishatheroadgyal
Kellie Battman
Kelly McWilliam (Koko Mack)
Kimberley Stubbs
Kirsty Mulheron
Kyle O'Regan
L J Rooney
Laura O'Malley
Lauren Bridie
Lauren Humphreys
Liana Isadora
LilySevs
Little Red Sonja
Lochenz
Lois Mac
Loren Tibby

Lostinagoodbookgirl Jords
Lottie F
Luce Austin
Lucy Dyer
Lucy's Libation
Lucy Taylor
Mazi Bonita
Megan Hall
Megan Rees
Metzie aka Joanna
Michelle Moorhouse
Mike Hailu
Monika Niemeier
Mslulubeth
Nadia AM Appointment
Nadine Hall
Natalie Hones
Nic Parks
Nick Hill
Nikki McGlead
Noëmi
Normins
October Alderson
Paul Gossip
Rachael Blair
Rachael Cooney
Rachael Sheldon
Rebecca Cox
Reekie-minaj
Rob Tinfoil
Rosie Toomey
Roxy Greene
Ruby Ettle

Ruth McDermott
Ruuuth
Sadie Cyanide
Sara Jayne
Sarah McPoland
Sasha Cheeky Zebra
Sel Demir
Serenity Yoga Cork
Shannon Fry
Sharma_86
Sharron Wormald
Shauna Jade
Shirls
Shivani
Siobhan Walters
Sofia Kasapi
Sophie Bee
Stacey Bicar
Stekodat
Stephanie Mathews
Stevie Lux
Susie Waine
Tash Dixon
Tia Marquis-Copeland
Tijeno
Vani the Kiwi
Vitnija Saldava
Whibley
www.thefeministshop.com
Yagmur
Yehbarley
Zaiera Leverette
Zosh Blue Moon

Glossary

Catfish – someone who pretends to be someone else online

Cis – Stonewall's definition is 'Someone whose gender identity is the same as the sex they were assigned at birth. Non-trans is also used by some people'

Fuckboy – a man who intentionally manipulates, deceives, controls and generally brings misery to the people he is romantically involved with

Gary – Gary is the generic name used for fuckboys

Ghosting – when someone disappears without trace or explanation

The ick – the ick is the feeling that hits when you go off someone to the point of repulsion. You are so turned off by them that you can barely stand to be in their company. It can hit for rational or irrational reasons. You cannot control the ick

Incel – a person who defines themselves as involuntarily celibate. They feel that they are being denied sex because they aren't a stereotypical 'jock' or 'lad'. They blame women for their lack of sex and are often deeply misogynistic

Intersectional feminism – intersectional feminism requires us to consider the implications of race, class, disability, sexuality, poverty and other such factors and how they intersect with gender inequality to create further oppression

Pegging – when a woman penetrates her male partner anally, with a sex toy, if she is cis

Pink flag – a signal that you may need to be extra alert for red flags. It is a warning to be cautious but not a danger warning. Several pink flags equal a red

Red flag – a danger warning. They can appear in someone's words, actions or behaviour

Situationship – a regular but casual relationship that isn't actually a relationship. A situationship is defined by the fact that feelings have become involved on one side only. One person usually ends up getting hurt or compromising their needs in order to keep the other one around

Spectacular buff ting – someone who loves themselves regardless of their flaws, failings and past mistakes

Wokefish – someone who pretends to have progressive political ideologies in order to attract partners under false pretences

Resources

Support services

These resources are all UK-based. If you are not in the UK, you can usually find targeted support via Google by searching for subject alongside your local area – for example, 'Domestic abuse support Warsaw Poland' or 'Rape survivors support Kingston Jamaica'.

In an emergency, or if you are in immediate danger, please contact the police.

Asian Women's Resources Centre: www.asianwomencentre.org.uk/ 0208 961 6549/5701

Free Your Mind CIC: www.freeyourmindcic.com

Galop LGBT+ domestic abuse helpline: 0207 704 2040

Irish Women's Aid: www.womensaid.ie

Jewish Women's Aid: www.jwa.org.uk/contact-us; domestic violence support line: 0808 801 0500; sexual violence support line: 0808 801 0656

Muslim Women's Network: www.mwnuk.co.uk/ 0800 999 5786

Paladin National Stalking Advocacy Service: www.paladinservice.co.uk/ 0203 866 4107

Prisoners' Families Helpline: www.prisonreformtrust.org.uk/ 0808 802 0060

Rape Crisis: www.rapecrisis.org.uk/ 0808 802 9999

Refuge 24-hour National Domestic Abuse Helpline: www.nationaldahelpline.org.uk/ 0808 200 0247

Relate relationship counselling: www.relate.org.uk

Respect Men's Advice Line (male survivors): www.mensadviceline.org.uk/ 0808 801 0327

Revenge Porn Helpline: www.revengepornhelpline.org.uk/ 0345 6000 459

Rights of Women: www.rightsofwomen.org.uk/ 0207 251 6575

Royal Voluntary Service: www.royalvoluntaryservice.org.uk/ 0330 555 0310

Scottish Women's Aid: www.womensaid.scot/ 0800 027 1234

Sistah Space (for African heritage women and girls): www.sistahspace.org.uk/ 0207 846 8350

Southall Black Sisters: www.southallblacksisters.org.uk/ 0208 571 9595

Survivors Trust: www.thesurvivorstrust.org/ 0808 801 0818

Victim Support: www.victimsupport.org.uk/ 0808 168 9111

Welsh Women's Aid: www.welshwomensaid.org.uk/ 0808 801 0800

Women's Aid: www.womensaid.org.uk

Mental health

In an emergency, please seek immediate help by calling an ambulance or seeking urgent support via the NHS.

The NHS has helpful information on how to access therapy. You can self-refer via your GP, though there is likely to be a waiting list. You can also access private therapy, some of which can be accessed for free, or at reduced rates. Check out the information on the NHS websites listed below.

www.nhs.uk/mental-health/talking-therapies-medicine-treatments/ talking-therapies-and-counselling/counselling/

www.nhs.uk/mental-health/talking-therapies-medicine-treatments/ talking-therapies-and-counselling/types-of-talking-therapies/

If you are going to access a private therapist, it is important to check the professional standards website: www.professionalstandards.org.uk/ check-practitioners

Black Minds Matter: www.blackmindsmatteruk.com
Co-Dependents Anonymous: www.codauk.org
LGBT+ Foundation: www.lgbt.foundation/ 0845 330 3030
Mind: www.mind.org.uk
Samaritans: www.samaritans.org/ 116 123 (freephone)
Sex and Love Addicts Anonymous: www.slaauk.org

Books

Sherry Argov, *Why Men Love Bitches* (New York, 2002)

Laura Bates, *Everyday Sexism* (London, 2014)

Laura Bates, *Men Who Hate Women* (London, 2020)

Russell Brand, *Recovery* (London, 2017)

Fran Bushe, *My Broken Vagina* (London, 2021)

Caroline Criado-Perez, *Invisible Women* (London, 2019)

Dr Karen Gurney, *Mind the Gap* (London, 2020)

Steve Harvey, *Act Like a Lady, Think Like a Man* (New York, 2019) (not recommended)

bell hooks, *All About Love* (New York, 2001)

bell hooks, *Ain't I a Woman?* (New York, 1987)

Helena Kennedy QC, *Misjustice – How British Law is Failing Women* (London, 2019)

Lindsay King-Miller, *Ask a Queer Chick* (New York, 2016)

Jo Langford, *The Pride Guide* (Lanham, 2018)

Amir Levine and Rachel S. F. Heller, *Attached* (New York, 2019)

Jen Sincero, *You are a Bad Ass* (New York, 2016)

Dr Jessica Taylor, *Why Women are Blamed for Everything* (London, 2021)

Naomi Wolf, *The Beauty Myth* (London, 1991)

Kimberlé Williams Crenshaw, *On Intersectionality: Essential Writings* (New York, 2022)

Jamie Windust, *In Their Shoes* (London, 2020)

Instagram accounts

@am.appointment
@clementine_ford
@doposupport
@dr.mayus
@drjesstaylor
@drnaomisutton
@honestly.im.ok
@jowestwood
@joysworldthepodcast
@justthetippod
@kelechnekoff
@megan_rose_lane
@muslimsexeducation

@my_boyfriend_has_herpes
@oloni
@salmaelwardany
@singleblackwoman_x
@survivorsfightingback
@thatsinglemum
@the.vulva.gallery
@thesexdoctor
@thirtysomethingsingle
@tindertranslators
@triplecripples
@wecantconsentto
@yung_pueblo

Podcasts

Call Her Daddy
Just the Tip
Laid Bare
LalalaLetMeExplain: Bad Dates, Good Stories, Naked Truths
Say Your Mind, Kelechi Okafor

TV

I May Destroy You (Michaela Coel, 2020)
Liberated: The New Sexual Revolution (Benjamin Nolot, 2017)

About the author

LalalaLetMeExplain is the anonymous relationships expert who delves into the highs and lows of modern-day dating to give raw and honest advice on topics that people are often too embarrassed or afraid to talk about. A qualified social worker and dating and relationships educator, she left her fifteen-year career in the public sector in 2018 to bring her professional knowledge to social media.

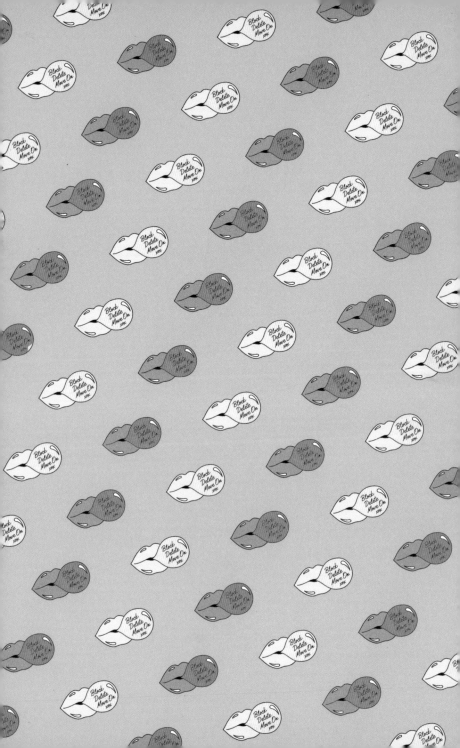